Jesus

A Dialogue with the Saviour

by Lev Gillet

"A Monk of the Eastern Church"

translated by a Monk of the Western Church

introduction by Louis Bouyer

icon illustrations by Mark Melone

**Educational Services
Diocese of Newton
West Newton, Ma 02165**

Jesus, A Dialogue with the Saviour is a translation from the second French edition:
Jesus, Simples Regards sur le Sauveur (Editions de Chevetogne)
Originally published 1963, Desclee Company, Tournai, Belgium
Paperback edition copyright 1965, Paulist Press, New York

Printed in the United States of America
Published by special arrangement with Paulist Press
All rights reserved

Library of Congress Cataloging-in-Publication Data

Gillet, Lev
[Jesus, simples regards sur le sauveur. English]
Jesus, a dialogue with the Saviour / by a monk of the Eastern Church; translated by a monk of the Western Church.
    p. cm.
Translation of Jesus, simples regards sur le sauveur. 2nd ed.
Reprint. Originally published: New York: Desclee Co., 1963.
ISBN 1-56125-016-3
1. Jesus Christ -- Meditations. I. Title.
BT268.G5413 1990
232--dc20   90-34081
                                                      CIP

To You Lord...

Foreword

Originally published in French by the Monastery of Chevetogne, Belgium, this book quickly met with world-wide success. Before its first English edition it had already appeared in German, Dutch, Spanish and Greek translations. No wonder, as the perception of the Gospel so evident in these pages is so clear and direct as to touch the hearts of people the world over.

The author of this work, the late Archimandrite Lev Gillet (1893-1980), used the pseudonym "monk of the Eastern Church" in several of his earlier works, painting his word-pictures as anonymously as any monastic iconographer. He was a figure who captured the imagination of many Europeans interested in the Eastern Churches and ecumenism during this century.

Bishop Kallistos of Diokleia (Timothy Ware), in his foreword to *The Jesus Prayer* (Crestwood, NY, St. Vladimir's Seminary Press: 1987), tenderly summarizes Father Lev's life and indicates further references on this remarkable individual. He writes, "What used to impress me most, as I listened to him, was the freshness that marked his interpretation of the Scripture. He took some familiar saying or incident from the Gospels - Jesus with the rich young man, with the Samaritan woman at the well, with the woman taken in adultery - and, as he commented on the well-known text, it was as if we were listening to the words of the Bible for the first time, as if we were ourselves part of the scene that he was describing."

The present volume presents the reflections of this "transparently evangelical" man in forty-six chapters. Yet a single paragraph is often sufficient to inspire us for some time. This is a book to be kept at hand - at home, at work, in the car - wherever we may have or need a moment to put aside the tasks of the day and allow the light of the Gospel to touch us. We are indebted to Father Philip Raczka and Saint Ann's Parish of West Paterson, New Jersey, hosts of our 1990 Diocesan Convention, for making this edition possible.

Rev. Fred Saato
Director of Educational Services
Eparchy of Newton

About the Icon Illustrations

The four icons each illustrate an important Scriptural image pointing to the mystery of the Lord Jesus, Son and Word of God:

Emmanuel (facing page 1) - The icon of Jesus as a young boy is traditionally associated with the prophetic words of Isaiah 7:14, "A young woman shall conceive and bear a son and call his name Emmanu-el, that is *God is with us*". At the incarnation of the divine Word, this prophecy is fulfilled to an unimaginable degree. The divine presence in Jesus is not simply as a protection from above or even as a life within by grace, but the very embodiment of the eternal God Himself: *"Before Abraham was, I am"* (Jn 8:58).

The Angel of Great Counsel (facing page 43) - The icon of the Word as an angel is connected with several Old Testament incidents: the trinity of angels who visit Abraham and Sara (Gen 18), the mysterious fourth man in the fiery furnace "like one of the gods" (Dan 3:25), and especially "the messenger of the convenant" (Mal 3:1). The Lord Jesus is His Father's messenger or angel to us, in that He came not in His own name, but unreservedly in the service of His Father. *"My food is to do the will of Him who sent me and to accomplish His work ... for I have come down from heaven, not to do my own will but the will of Him who sent me"* (Jn 4:34, 6:38).

The Wisdom of God (facing page 93) - The Great Church at Constantinople, Agia Sophia (the Holy Wisdom), had as its patronal icon the Pantocrator: the Lord enthroned between the Theotokos and the Forerunner. Incarnate in the flesh, He is the personification of the secret and hidden wisdom of what God has prepared for those who love Him (cf 1 Cor 1,2). The Lord Jesus Himself spoke of Wisdom in this way (Luke 11:49 - "Therefore also the Wisdom of God said, ...") but it is only in the Spirit that we recognize who that Wisdom actually is: *"Christ: the power of God and the wisdom of God"* (1 Cor 1:24).

In Another Form (facing page 137) - When the risen Christ appeared to the two disciples on the Emmaus road, they did not recognize Him, the Scriptures say, because "He appeared in another form" (Mk 16:12). Christ was not resuscitated - brought back to His previous life - but risen in glory to a new and transfigured life. In this He is "the first fruits of those who have fallen asleep" (1 Cor 15:20), for we are all called to share this glory with Him. For this reason the Emmaus icon is often placed behind the Holy Table, where we receive the mystical foretaste of eternity, where *He "will change our lowly body to be like His glorious body"* (Phil 3:21).

INTRODUCTION

Among all the books which are published every day, we should consider as priceless those which renew for us our acquaintance with Jesus. Such books are rare. Not because a great deal is not written about Him. But because even the most scholarly research of the historian, the most profound speculations of the theologian, to say nothing of art and literature, often prove incapable of revealing Him.

The bulk of the commentaries is such that one is tempted to bow to them without even catching a glimpse of their content. And it must be avowed that when we approach them nevertheless, too often they burden us and bar our way to Him much more than they open it for us.

A book which does not confine itself to speaking *about* Jesus, which does not make us dizzy from a lot of tittle-tattle serving only to distract us from speaking to Him ourselves and all the more from hearing Him, is a very rare thing indeed. Yet it seems that such a book has just appeared.

It is a mysterious book originally published in French by the monks of Chevetogne, that dual-rite monastery in Belgium dedicated to the reunion of Christendom, and whose founder Dom Lambert Beauduin has only recently gone to his reward.

This little volume does not even bear the author's name. We are only told that a monk of the Eastern Church wrote it.

But as soon as you open these pages, you will experience the same impression as you would on opening a vessel of sacred chrism in an Eastern Rite Church. You are surrounded by a heavenly fragrance whose freshness, purity and simplicity are retained in the most exquisite, indivisible mixture of countless flowers.

Some forty short meditations, without any apparent order, recapture the words and scenes of the Gospel. There is no eloquence, no dissertation, no evocation whatever to bog them down. Rather, we find always a direct contact with the soul of the Saviour who speaks to the soul of the reader. "Follow thou Me!" This statement, about which the anonymous writer of these pages has some very decisive words, pervades everything he says.

This contemplative monk has meditated and lived the Gospel (he himself intimates this to the reader) in the holy places of Judea, all along the roads of Galilee. But do not think that he is going to waste his time and ours in some romantic evocation! By simply following, as he does, the steps of Christ, he has been helped (and he helps us) to rediscover that very springing forth of the Word who touches hearts and pierces through them. From a stony heart which belongs to all ages of sinful humanity, He recreates that heart of flesh of which Ezechiel speaks.

We suspect at every page, almost at every line, a refined culture in the one who, though stripped of everything, though poor with Christ who made Himself poor, speaks in such a way (without ever raising his voice) — with such a discreet voice that Jesus Himself does not have to reject it in order to speak to us directly. The language which is so wonderfully dense and transparent is sufficient to prove it. Very quickly one becomes aware that this man has read every book. Yet these books could not hold him back, because through them, as through all things and beyond all things, he was only looking for the One whose call he had heard and which he makes us hear too.

Our pretentious and complicated apostolates create for us the false impression that the man of today cannot hear Christ without all kinds of explanations, rearrangements and especially without endless preparation. Here we have a solitary who is able to make every man hear Christ from the very first word, simply by taking His own words again, but taking them from lips where only the name of Jesus has succeeded in saying everything.

Cast aside all your ponderous, wordy books and read this one. As soon as you have opened it, your whole house, as the Gospel says, will be filled with the odor of sweetness.

Louis Bouyer, Cong. Or.

✥

                     To You, Lord Jesus,
I humbly dedicate these thoughts which have developed during the course of so many years, on the very roads which You have travelled in the days of Your earthly life and in the very city in which You suffered. They are the fruit of Jerusalem and of the Sea of Galilee and the fruit of almost a whole lifetime.

    Why add a drop of water to that ocean of books which speak about You? I shall venture to say in all simplicity: it is because I felt that You were telling me, also, to speak about You. " Return to thy house and tell them..." [1] *And the possessed man whom You cured in the country of the Gerasenes*

----

[1] Lk 8, 39.

went away and began to announce everything You aid for him and how You had pity on him.

It was my hope that, by sharing with others what had been given to me, I would perhaps help a few souls. I have tried to say, in stuttering language, what became clear to me when I fixed my gaze on You and what I seemed to hear when I became silent in order to hear Your voice. There are many things which one could expect to find here but of which I have not spoken. I only wanted to describe, O my Saviour, a few aspects of Your face, a few moments of personal conversation with You, a few phases of a very personal experience. I could not, I would not aspire to anything else. I sometimes had the impression — I ought to say it only with trepidation — that certain words, certain ideas came to me from a distance and from a height far beyond me. Lord, have pity on a poor sinner who has ventured to speak about You without having cleansed his lips with the flaming coal.

I know that my words are of no value, are nothing. The only result I wish for is to touch a few souls and to lead them to You. Lord, lead those who will read my words to the point where abandoning these pages, they will open again, or perhaps for the first time, Your Gospel, — to the point where in silence they will allow Your word to enter their hearts.

✦ *I*

The Gospel begins with the Genealogy of Jesus Christ.[1] What does this long list of Hebrew names mean? For the Jews, the necessity of underlining the descent of the Messias from David. Another meaning is that in this lineage there are murderers, adulterers and incestuous persons. If Jesus is born in my soul, He is born there in spite of and through the accumulation of my sins. Jesus pierces, finds His way through my faults, climbing over them one after the other. It is His genealogy in me. In this break-through shines forth His mercy, His condescension, also His strength.

[1] Mt 1, 1.

Mary, bearing the child in her womb, and Joseph, are on their way to be registered at Bethlehem. [1] It is not at Rome, nor at Athens, nor at Jerusalem that Jesus wished to be born. So we can find the mystery of Jesus' birth only in the poor Judean village. We must go up to Bethlehem, become citizens of Bethlehem, acquire — no, achieve — the humble spirit of Bethlehem.

The angels do not simply say to the shepherds that a Saviour *is* born. They say: " This day is born to *you* a Saviour. " [2] Jesus is born for each one of the shepherds. His birth remains for each one of us a very personal event; Jesus is a gift offered to every man.

There is no room in the inn for Mary who is bearing Jesus, nor for Joseph. [3] There is no place in the inn of this world for a disciple of the Master. What dangerous comfort, if I succeed in getting a place for myself there! What do the inn and the manger have in common?

The Magi, divinely warned in a dream, return to their country by another road. [4] They must avoid Herod. In the spiritual

[1] Lk 2, 3. [2] Lk 2, 11.
[3] Lk 2, 7. [4] Mt 2, 12.

sense, he whom God has led to the crib can certainly go back home, to his own country, to his house; but it will be by another road. That is to say, the motives, the attitudes, the manner of existing, the means used, can no longer be the same. When one has gone to Bethlehem, a radical change takes place.

It had been revealed to Simeon that he would not die without seeing the Saviour.[1] Oh! how much I should like to have such a guarantee! Not to die without seeing Jesus — not to see Him with the eyes of the body, but to see Him (to really see Him) with the eyes of faith! After my death, I hope to see Him differently.

To Simeon was granted more than to see Jesus. He held the child in his arms.[2] Lord, let me embrace spiritually the little child.

The angel orders Joseph to take the child and his mother and flee into Egypt.[3] There are times when, because we are too weak, it is better to fly from danger, to draw apart from it. But we must take with us what is more precious: take Jesus, take the child in His smallness, in His own weakness, who will

[1] Lk 2, 26.   [2] Lk 2, 28.
[3] Mt 2, 13.

strengthen us in our own weakness. With Him we must take His mother, as the beloved disciple took her, after the ninth hour. The mystery of Mary is inseparable from the mystery of Jesus : a mystery of mercy and affection.

✣ *II*

"We would see Jesus,"[1] certain Greeks said to the apostle Philip. And it is always just this prayer which I address to the Holy Spirit. O Lord Holy Spirit, make me see Jesus!

The pure of heart will see God.[2] The sermon on the Mount makes it quite plain And Jesus can be seen only by the pure of heart, who can move directly to the very heart of the Gospel. For them, it is very simple. But it is difficult for those whose gaze is troubled by the passions or by the unbridled quest for purely human knowledge. They

[1] Jn 12, 21.
[2] Mt 5, 8.

must re-learn purity of heart in order to regain the direct, immediate gaze of Jesus.

I learn to look at Jesus in so far as I learn to be looked at by Him, that is, to submit myself to His gaze. Before speaking to Simon Peter [1] at the time of his first call, Jesus looks at him, and the Greek word implies that He looks at him with insistence. The same insistent gaze was again cast upon Simon Peter, [2] when Jesus was coming out of Caiphas' house and Peter denied Him. The first of such looks from Jesus fills the disciple with joy and light. The second makes the disciple who has failed his Master weep bitterly. There are looks of the Saviour which cause weeping: without them, I shall not deserve to have the glance of light cast upon me.

The conditions for the vision are the same as those imposed by Jesus on the three disciples [3] whom He made witnesses of His transfiguration. Jesus " took them with Him "; He " led " them; He led them " up a high mountain, " where they were " alone, apart. " Let us consider being alone with Jesus, letting ourselves be led by Him. The ascent is painful

[1] Mt 4, 18. [2] Lk 22, 61.
[3] Mt 17, 1.

— far above what is bad or mediocre in our life. Ordinarily all these conditions remain necessary. (I say " ordinarily " because there are exceptional cases : Saul on the road to Damascus.) [1]

The theme is still purity of heart. The pure heart is unalloyed (as one speaks of gold which is pure), an undivided heart, an unshared heart, its integrity preserved — or recovered. Impurity, in the sexual sense, is only one of the forms of disintegration. " My son, give me thy heart, " [2] said Wisdom in the Old Testament. Only a heart that is " given " can grasp Jesus; but it must be given without turning back, complete, without fault. The one is opposed to the many. " My name is Legion, " [3] answered the man possessed, when Jesus asked his name.

My child, you have sought your own happiness. Instead of the happiness which you were seeking, I offer you My beatitudes. Your whole life has made it clear to you that your road was closed to you, outside of the complete giving of yourself. Blessed are you to whom I have barred the roads which are not Mine!

[1] Acts 9, 3.   [2] Prv 23, 26.
[3] Mk 5, 9.

When I look at You, Lord Jesus, I no longer feel the need of questioning You, of receiving answers to specific questions. Your person, Your image are a sufficient and complete answer. If I fix my eyes on You, in You everything is revealed to me, obscurely, indeed, but powerfully; and even this obscurity (which between us, cannot *not* be) is often a dazzling brightness. When it seems to me that I have obtained a clear vision of You, everything becomes clear to me.

Your word, Lord Jesus, is not a commentary on a relationship which should exist between You and me. Your word gives birth to that relationship. It does not inform me of Christ's behaviour; it establishes my vital contact with it. It is the very irruption of the divine behaviour in my life.

Every one of the Saviour's words is a declaration of His grace. In Jesus, even in His most everyday remarks, it is the Redeemer who speaks. The shadow of the cross falls on all things. No, the sunlight of the cross!

✠ III

Jesus is the truth. In Him is all truth. In so far as the truth which is in Jesus is discovered, all truth is discovered. This can be applied to the science, art and culture of men. We must see the world with the Saviour's eyes.

The Saviour gives no direct answer, either affirmative or negative, to John's disciples who questioned Him about His mission. He tells them to report to John what they have seen.[1] Jesus charged Peter, who gave a sound answer and confessed the Messias, not to reveal the mystery publicly.[2] Every man has to discover

[1] Mt 11, 4.
[2] Mt 16, 20.

for himself the secret of Jesus. And even if we learn from others who Jesus is, and even if the others are commissioned to teach this to us, it is only by an intensely personal experience that we shall come to know what Jesus is.

In fact, of the many souls who believed all they must believe, and who led a just and pious life, we may wonder : did this soul know the Saviour? Did he know Him intimately, as one can know one's closest friend, as a man and woman who love each other can know each other, as alone He can be known who is more spiritual than ourselves? A number of acquired notions (and also true ones) concerning the Saviour are often substituted for a personal and intense knowledge of the Saviour. It can be a hindrance just like a screen between Jesus and us. Lord, do I really know You, or do I only know what I have read about You, what I have heard about You?

Jesus does not want the soul to be fastened onto the vision granted momentarily and to be limited by it. Nathaniel saw Jesus and he believed. But Jesus said to him : " Greater things than these shalt thou see. "[1] The joy of the vision must not interrupt its drive. It

[1] Jn 1, 50.

must stimulate its continuance. We must keep on perpetually seeking Jesus. " Seek, and you shall find. "[1] Yes. But also : because you have found, you will seek further. We shall cease to look for Jesus only at the end of time. The discovery of Jesus will not exhaust our search for Him as long as we have not obtained the final vision. St. Augustine says it : *Quaeramus inventum*, let us search after Him who has been found.

[1] Mt 7, 7.

✠ *IV*

Must we see Jesus? More than that: we must touch Him. " Which we have seen with our eyes, and our hands have handled, of the word of life...," [1] writes the apostle John. The woman afflicted with an issue of blood declared [2] that if only she could touch Jesus' garments, she would be healed. She touched timorously, from behind, Jesus' tunic; and she was cured of her illness. I ask that no day pass without my being able to touch at least the fringe of Jesus' garment without a power going out from the Saviour which will be unto me a pledge of salvation.

[1] 1 Jn 1, 1.
[2] Mt 9, 20.

We must touch Jesus in secret conversation with Him, in contact with the human members of the Body of Christ which is the Church, in the mystery of the Lord's Last Supper. We must not suppose that we have touched Jesus because we have drawn near to Him. But there are privileged moments when a kind of ineffable shudder, a sort of irrestible evidence (which, if authentic, cast us into the depths of humility) make us cry out : " I have just touched Jesus, " or better, " Jesus has just touched me. " Lord, I am not worthy to lift my eyes towards You. Be merciful to me, a sinner. [1]

How the facts of Christ's life perplex us! Never are they exactly what we are expecting. And yet they go even further and are more positive than we were expecting. Joseph of Arimathea [2] buried Jesus, but Jesus is He whom no sepulchre can contain or restrain. The women bring aromatic spices [3] to the tomb; now it is a God already risen whom they plan to anoint. A woman breaks a jar of perfume [4] on the Lord's living body, in order to give Him glory; now Jesus says that it is with a view to His burial that she performed this act. The

[1] Lk 18, 13.
[2] Mt 27, 59.
[3] Mk 16, 1.
[4] Mt 26, 12.

cross seems to destroy hope, but the resurrection destroys despair. The divine acts, which ruin our plans, go beyond either hope or despair. Thus it is with each of Jesus' interventions in our personal life. Every one of them makes something explode, but also makes flight possible. Jesus won't fit into any of our plans. His presence, His word break every bound.

✠ V

"Learn of Me..."[1] We cannot know Jesus without learning Jesus. We must learn day by day, hour by hour, little by little; it is a task of docility and perseverance. It supposes a daily familiarity with Jesus : being close to Him, listening to Him. " Of Me... " The Saviour desires this direct, intimate relation with each soul. Others can prepare us for His message and tell us it again with profit. But these will never be anything but tutors. He alone is the Master, the one whose teaching springs from the Godhead. Here the teaching is united with the teacher. To receive Jesus, message is to discover the person of the Master.

[1] Mt 11, 29.

Jesus wants to reveal to us what He is. And what does He want us to learn about Him? This, which is very simple, very brief and accessible to the most ordinary and ignorant people: "that I am meek and humble of heart."[1] That is what He wants us to know first of all. Is it very much? Cloaked in these words we could discover Bethlehem and Golgotha.

To know Jesus we must be capable of a certain disinterest and a sort of sacred objectivity. This knowledge must be the greatest interest of our life. Therefore we must prevent our lives, even on the spiritual plane, from becoming our primary occupation. What we will learn about Jesus from Jesus must be more precious to us, more desirable, than what we will learn about ourselves. Because the Saviour's face forces us to become aware at once of our own proportions, of our own situation; from this immediately emanates the possibility — more : the active power — of our metamorphosis. But Jesus' face must not interest us primarily because of its effects on us. First of all, we must be captivated by its intrinsic beauty.

[1] Mt 11, 29.

"Have I been so long a time with you and have you not known me, Philip?"[1] My child, I have been with you also for so many years! Yet, in many respects, I am unknown to you. What you know about Me is nothing compared to what there is yet for you to learn. Are you willing to devote the time which is left to you to knowing Me?

This is the knowledge of Christ: " eternal life, that they may know Thee, the only true God, and Jesus Christ whom Thou hast sent."[2] It is not enough to say that this knowledge takes place in eternal life. It *is* eternal life. Eternal life consists in this. Consequently, eternal life begins here below. This knowledge is the link between time and eternity. The only true God and Jesus Christ whom He has sent: they are not two objects of knowledge. For it is only in Jesus that we know His Father and His Spirit. " He that seeth me seeth the Father also."[3]

---

[1] Jn 14, 9.　　[2] Jn 17, 3.
[3] Jn 14, 9.

✣ *VI*

The man who gives himself entirely to a work, either for the purpose of assimilating or of developing another's work, or of elaborating a particular work of his own, that man restricts himself, simplifies himself, unifies himself. He is wrapped up, so to speak, in the work to which he applies himself. It is the same for the man who wants to know Jesus. We must shut ourselves up in Jesus, we must include in Him all other people, everything else. Thereby, invisibly, our knowledge will gush forth in grace upon the world.

My Saviour, I have enough to consider and to discuss concerning You. I have read enough, listened enough, spoken enough. I should like simply to come close to You. Allow me to close the books. Let nothing stand between us any longer. Let me come to You. Let me be absorbed, engulfed in Your presence. May Your heart alone speak to my heart!

Lord Jesus, how could my heart listen to Your heart while the Doctors and Scribes are wrangling about Your name? Is the noise of their voices not going to drown out what you said softly in secret? I repeat the words of Mary in the garden : " They have taken away my Lord; and I know not where they have laid Him. Tell me where thou hast laid Him and I will take Him away. "[1] I also would carry You away, Lord Jesus, carry You far from the tumults of the schools, far from the disputes of the wise men, far also from the bitter zealousness and contentions among the disciples (" Which of us is the greatest? ").[2] Let me adore You, see You, speak with You.

This presence, this intimacy which I long for, I can obtain from You, O Lord. You can appear to me without this new presence having a direct connection with the past. You can

[1] Jn 20, 13-15.
[2] Lk 22, 24.

also make present and real and new for me the life which was Your earthly life. You can Yourself write in my soul a " Life of Jesus," old and new at the same time. Lord, reveal Yourself to me as the Jesus of the Gospel and as Jesus my contemporary.

✤ *VII*

Let us consider Christ Jesus in our age. Every word of a Gospel account is for me a present-day event. (It is also prolonged right up to eternal life.) It is quite different from a past event which I commemorate. It is for me, at this very moment, a conscious fact, belonging to my life. The Saviour's acts and words are linked to history in this sense, that they have an historical context and have taken place in time. But they go beyond time and history, as the God-Man transcends all human limits. Being of the past, they are, however, free of the past. They are contemporary with every man. And they open out to us the future.

Of John's two disciples who followed Him in silence, Jesus asks: " *What* seek you? " They answer: " Master, where dwellest *Thou*? " [1] They are not looking for something but for someone, a person. Furthermore, they wish to know, not only where Jesus is going, but where He dwells. We must desire a fixed, permanent way of life, close to Jesus, more than a passing encounter. Thus, from the first page, the history of the apostles puts Jesus at the center of things. What I am seeking is not moral perfection, nor is it a conception of the coherent or enticing world. It is not even this or that gift, this or that special divine grace, it is the person of Christ.

The question which Jesus asked the soldiers who came to arrest Him — " Whom seek ye? " [2] — recalls the question asked of the first two disciples: " What seek you? " [3] The expression " all seek for Thee, " [4] addressed one day to Jesus by the disciples, does not cease to be current. Some seek Jesus in order to join Him, others in order to render Him powerless. If only these two groups were distinctly separate! Alas! in our condition of sinful men we belong intermittently to one or the other group.

[1] Jn 1, 38.
[2] Jn 18, 4.
[3] Jn 1, 38.
[4] Mk 1, 37.

Jesus did not say: "I am showing you the way." He said: "I am the way." He did not say, "I am teaching you the truth"; He said, "I am the truth." He did not say, "I am giving you life"; He said, "I am the life."[1] St. Paul will often speak of Christ in like terms: Christ *is* my life,[2] He *is* our sanctification, our justice.[3] We can speak of Christ in substantives, because He is the very substance of all good things, of all gifts.

In Jesus a living person has replaced the law. It is no longer because of a written commandment that I shall shun murder and adultery, but because a person, Jesus Christ, has spoken, has lived and died in a way which henceforth constitutes the eternal model. Jesus abolishes and at the same time perfects the law.[4] Like the river which flows into the sea, each drop of water which was in the river maintains its existence in the womb of the sea, but the river, as a river, no longer exists.

For anyone who has understood this substitution, there is a specifically Christian way of bringing up problems in Christ. When Paul puts the Christians on guard against fornication,

[1] Jn 14, 6.
[2] Phil 1, 21.
[3] 1 Cor 1, 30.
[4] Mt 5, 17.

he is not indulging in moral considerations about purity; he only asks if the members of Christ are going to make themselves members of a prostitute.[1] He is not speaking of the immortality of the soul, but he says that, if Jesus has not risen from the dead, our hope is in vain.[2]

[1] 1 Cor 6, 15.
[2] 1 Cor 15, 14.

✠ *VIII*

In Christ Jesus the way and its end are identified. If we enter into the way which is Christ we have already obtained our objective. Whatever the problem may be, whether it be one of the lofty questions of the spiritual order or one of the simplest everyday problems, by embracing Jesus, by uniting ourselves more intimately to Him, we arrive at a solution. That does not dispense us either from reflection or from the appropriate methods, but our thinking will do its work in the light of Christ.

Some concrete problem confronts me — a serious decision to make, a difficult interview, a letter to write, personal relations, professional duties, etc. — O Lord, what ought I to do?

My child, *first of all*, unite yourself to Me. Be assured that in Me your personal problem is resolved. If you really see Me, you shall see the solution through Me, as it were transparently. Make use of your reasoning powers, but in My light and depending on My heart.

Martha believes that her brother will rise again on the last day. Jesus answers her: "I am the resurrection."[1] There are two teachings in this statement: the resurrection is not a purely eschatological reality, projected into the ultimate future. The resurrection is, in a very definite way, a reality already given; it already exists. It is the Saviour Himself who from now on is the cause and the power of the resurrection of the dead. Not by imagination, or memory, but by union with Christ, we join, at this very moment, those whom we have loved and who have left this world.

This union with the person of Christ is only possible if we set up before us, if we carry within ourselves, an intensely real image of Jesus. An image does not mean imagination nor a mental picture (although at the beginning that can be useful), but a definite interior vision,

[1] Jn 11, 25.

with hazy definition, which cannot be described outwardly.

Peter walks on the water.[1] As long as he looks at Jesus, as long as he goes towards Him, he is able to walk on the waves of the lake. But when he looks about him, when he notices that the wind is strong, he is struck with fear. He begins to sink. Jesus has to stretch forth His hand to save him.

If Peter had paid no attention to the waves and wind, if he had concentrated his gaze on Jesus alone, he would not have found himself in danger. His faith would not have been shaken.

In this you have also the cause of my falls. If I were capable of looking at Jesus alone, if I did not give way to consideration of danger or temptation, begin a kind of dialogue with them, I too would be able to walk on the water. All my faults originate by a fading or disappearance of the Saviour's image.

But how do I set up before me an image of Jesus strong enough to prevail over the fear of danger or the enticement of sin? Such an image is not the work of one minute or of one day. It is the work of months, of years, of

[1] Mt 14, 29.

a whole lifetime. A hasty, superficial image of Jesus is as one drawn on water. It vanishes with the first breeze, with the first jolt. I have to form this image of Jesus slowly and deeply, or rather, I must develop and then preserve a certain docility so that Jesus might engrave His face on my heart.

The beauty of the Saviour's face does not only attract, it acts and transforms. If our interior gaze is persistent, the Saviour's beauty touches us deeply, in proportion to this persistency.

O Lord, show me Your face;[1] and all my difficulties will melt like snow in the sunlight. Contemplating Your face, we shall be absorbed in Your light, lifted up from brightness to brightness, changed into Your image.

---

[1] Mt 17, 2.

✢ *IX*

Coming down from the mountain of transfiguration, the disciples see no one but " Jesus only. "[1] The obvious meaning of the phrase is: they no longer see Moses, Elias and the divine glory; they join Jesus once again under His everyday appearance. Another meaning can be added to this one: the soul which has been dazzled by the Saviour's light sees this same light over all beings: through men and things, it sees " Jesus only. "

Jesus calls souls individually. This is very pronounced in the Saviour's call to the first

[1] Mt 17, 8.

disciples. A deeply personal element enters into this call.

Jesus sees Simon,[1] and at once He tells him that he will become Cephas, the rock. Jesus sees Nathanael,[2] and immediately He says that here is an *Israelite* in whom there is no room for guile (Jacob, after first resorting to fraud, had become the sincere *Israel*). In Nathanael's case, it is the present state of soul of the newcomer which provides a theme for the Master's welcome. In Simon's case — and it is the most frequent — the Master foresees what the spiritual growth of the disciple will be. He accepts what the disciple will be, rather than what he is; He draws up even then an outline of his future ministry.

Jesus says to Nathanael: " Before that Philip called thee, when thou wast under the fig-tree, I saw thee."[3] We do not know to what episode Jesus is alluding. Had Nathanael retired under a fig-tree in a moment of prayer, or of meditation, or of temptation, or of interior struggle, or perhaps in a state of sin and repentance? What is certain is that the shadow of this fig-tree marks a decisive moment

[1] Jn 1, 42. [2] Jn 1, 47.
[3] Jn 1, 48.

in Nathanael's life. Jesus, at that moment of decision, was invisibly present, as He is present during the struggle which each one of us wages, under *our* fig-tree.

Under another fig-tree, four centuries later, Augustine will hear a voice say to him: *Tolle, lege*, " take and read. " This call will be decisive in his conversion. There are sterile fig-trees which Jesus curses,[1] which deceive by bearing leaves. There are exceptionally fertile fig-trees which Jesus blesses. Their fruits are Nathanael and Augustine.

The Master's call — whether it concerns Nathanael or each one of us — has secret and deep roots in what is most intimate about our life. " When thou wast under the fig-tree... "[2]

Peter's words, " Depart from me, for I am a sinful man, O Lord, "[3] is as essential in our relations with Jesus as that other of the apostle's sayings: " Bid me come to Thee upon the waters. "[4] These statements, one of humility and one of confidence, should be pronounced at the same time. But, in our condition of sinful and justified men, condemned and saved, there is room now for one of these statements, now for the other, alternating them.

[1] Mt 21, 19.
[2] Jn 1, 48.
[3] Lk 5, 8.
[4] Mt 14, 28.

" Come and see, "[1] says Jesus to the first two disciples, who asked Him where He dwells. " Come and see, "[2] says Philip to Nathanael, when he wants to bring him to the Master. These two moments were needed in order to attain Jesus. First of all, we must make a personal effort. Vision is the crown of this effort. Indeed our initial effort is itself a grace, a gift which emanates from the Saviour.

There are also moments of great distress when it is we who, like the Jews near Lazarus' tomb, cry out to Jesus: " Lord, come and see. "[3] Our act of faith is an answer to the Saviour's first invitation when He used the very same words.

---

[1] Jn 1, 39. [2] Jn 1, 46.
[3] Jn 11, 34.

✠ X

On only two occasions does the Gospel tell us that Jesus was surprised at something. In both cases it is a question of faith.

The first episode happened at Nazareth, when Jesus returns there. He is teaching in the synagogue. Neither His person nor His message are accepted. That is why He cannot perform any great miracle there. " And He wondered because of their unbelief. "[1]

The second episode occurred at Capharnaum. The Roman centurion is pleading for the cure of his paralyzed servant. " I will come

[1] Mk 6, 6.

and cure him," [1] says Jesus. The centurion protests: " I am not worthy that Thou shouldst enter under my roof; but only say the word." [2] When Jesus heard the centurion, " He marvelled." [3] He cures the servant from a distance; and He declares that even in Israel He has not found such great faith.

Let us compare these two episodes. There is something surprising here. The people of Nazareth are Israelites, having the law and the prophets, a precise belief and ritual. The centurion is a stranger to the people of the covenant (at most, perhaps a proselyte). Nonetheless, Jesus is amazed at the incredulity of Nazareth, and He is amazed at the centurion's faith. Nazareth's orthodoxy is not the living faith, the saving faith. If such a faith had animated them, the men of Nazareth would have opened their hearts to Jesus. They abide by a precise and fruitless religion. Their hearts remain closed. We do not know exactly what the centurion's faith may have been. He did not know about Jesus what we have been given to know, but he opened his heart to Jesus. He suspects in Him a Saviour and

---

[1] Mt 8, 7.   [2] Mt 8, 8.
[3] Mt 8, 10.

a Lord. His faith is based on confidence and obedience — not on sentimentality. It is an impulse of his whole being. He has no doubt that Jesus can and will cure his sick servant. In some way he stakes his life on Jesus' word. " Only say the word... "[1] : a humble and fervent expectation.

We know now what Jesus calls unbelief, and we know what He calls faith, " ...such great faith. "

Jesus sees what is in us. Does He find in us the centurion's faith or Nazareth's incredulity? At what would Jesus be amazed : at our faith — or at our unbelief?

" I do believe. Help my unbelief. "[2] Is not this antithesis, this paradoxical cry which the father of a possessed child calls out to Jesus, the phrase which suits our own situation?

We must believe in Jesus Christ : but why? Each one of us must render an account of his reasons for believing. There are as many roads which lead to Jesus as there are men.

As for me, Lord Jesus, I am one of those who believe in You because of Yourself. I believe in You because, with the help of Your

[1] Mt 8, 8.
[2] Mk 9, 23.

grace, no image within me can replace or wipe out Your image and because no word, as much as Yours, can penetrate to the very depths of my heart. I believe in You because You have made me know the beauty of Your face. I believe in You because — to use the words of the officer sent to arrest You — " never did man speak like this man. " [1] I believe in You because, for me, outside of You, there is nothing.

---

[1] Jn 7, 46.

THE ANGEL OF GREAT COUNSEL

✠ *XI*

      The atmosphere of Jesus is luminous. " I am the light of the world. "[1] With Jesus there is no trace of clouds or storm, of pathos and tempestuous violence, of darkness rent by lightning flashes. There is not even a partial shadow. Everything in Jesus is crystal clear. This clarity does not exclude an often keen sharpness.

      There is no tragedy about Jesus, because no problem remains without a solution. The disciple's difficulty is not to be ignorant of what he must do, but to have the strength to do it. What is called the tragedy of human existence disappears when confronted by the

[1] Jn 8, 12.

pure light of Christ. If we see the light, we can walk in the light.

During the transfiguration, Christ's garments became "shining" and "exceeding white as snow, so as no fuller upon earth can whiten."[1] The vision of Jesus — and even the image which we form of Him in ourselves — is inseparable from that impression of light, of whiteness, of dazzling purity.

Jesus has the vastness of the sea, of a deep-blue sea at nightfall, of a sea which the noonday sun covers with a blinding whiteness. On the horizon the sealine and the skyline merge. In this way, Lord, as far as my gaze is able to follow You, I see You lost in the glory of the Father.

What happened at the transfiguration? The Master, who lived with His disciples and to whose appearance they were accustomed, seems to them to be suddenly transformed, wrapped in light, radiant. To us also it is sometimes given to experience a certain impression of Jesus which is entirely new and overwhelming. We are not speaking of that corporeal vision of the Saviour which has been the privilege of some — perhaps even of many —

[1] Mk 9, 2.

throughout the centuries. It happens, however, sometimes, that the Saviour's presence is imposed on us, cast on us and takes hold of us. We feel His light without seeing it, or rather, we suspect it. Thus does the morning sun filter across a sleeper's closed eyes. The Master, whose daily appearance is so meek and humble, [1] makes us tremble when we come in contact with His power. Such are moments of transfiguration.

The Jews knew no divine light other than the pillar of fire [2] which guided Israel into the desert. This was a limited, temporary light, the light for one people and for one era. Jesus proclaims Himself the light " of the world, " the eternal, universal light which " enlighteneth every man that cometh into this world. " [3] Blessed are You, O Lord, because Your light works in all souls and because (however distorted it may be) it is to be found in all races, in all religious beliefs.

---

[1] Mt 11, 29. [2] Ex 13, 21.
[3] Jn 1, 9.

✥   *XII*

" He made that twelve should be with Him and that He might send them to preach. "¹ The first mark of the apostolate is to have been with Jesus. The consignment into the mission field is subordinate to this first condition. But it is not enough for the apostles to be close to Jesus. He wants to " have " them with Him. One thing is the fact of His simple presence, another thing the fact of being in the hands of Jesus as His possession, as matter, into which He breathes life and shapes it.

¹ Mk 3, 14.

The servant of the High Priest asks Peter: "Did not I see thee in the garden with Him?"[1] Was I with Jesus (am I still with Him) in the garden, on the Mount of Olives?

"I will that, where I am, they also whom thou hast given Me may be with Me."[2] Jesus is speaking of Heaven where His disciples will see His glory. The words, however, are subject to a more general sense. The disciple must be everywhere where the Master is. Am I with Jesus — by reliving these episodes in my soul — there where He was present during His earthly life? Am I with Him in the places and moments where He is present today?

Consider His coming. "I will come again,"[3] Jesus said after the Last Supper. This must not be taken merely in a future sense. The coming of Christ is not something in the future, it is continually present. I hear the Saviour's footsteps on the road, near my door. "Behold, I stand at the gate and knock."[4] He comes today; He comes at this very hour. He comes; He comes forever.

Jesus comes up to the disciples who are going to Emmaus and goes along the way with

---

[1] Jn 18, 26.
[2] Jn 17, 24.
[3] Jn 14, 3.
[4] Ap 3, 20.

them. But their eyes are " held that they should not know Him. "[1] It is in this way that Jesus is with us on all our roads. Whether I walk on the city streets or on the country paths, Jesus is there with me. He is there in a most real way, by the universal presence of His divine nature, and although Christ's glorified body is next to the Father, the Saviour's human nature, by virtue of its bond with the divine nature, prolongs and extends to us in some way the effects of His presence in Heaven and becomes accessible. I can say : " He walks with me, close to me. " I can see Him with the eyes of faith. In that is an experience at every possible moment of Christ's presence. I am never alone, neither in my room nor outside the house. Jesus is always with me. I can always listen to Him; I can always converse with Him.

" Was not our heart burning within us whilst He spoke in the way? "[2]

---

[1] Lk 24, 16.
[2] Lk 24, 32.

✠ *XIII*

" Come ye after Me. "[1]
This is the most customary form of the call which Jesus gives to those who will be His disciples.

We must follow Jesus. First of all, we must not be where Jesus is not, nor go where He would not go. Next, we must go where He is going, and go with Him. We must not follow at a distance, but close by Him; not aiming at outdistancing Him and going faster than He. We must walk humbly behind Him.

We must not be preoccupied with anything else but following. " What is it to thee?

[1] Mt 4, 19.

Follow thou Me." [1] What will become of John does not concern Peter; what concerns Peter is only to follow Jesus.

My child, you are anxious about many people and many things. You are anxious about your very life, about what you have undertaken, but I have asked you for only one thing, a thing so simple: to follow Me.

The Saviour's first two disciples having left the Baptist follow their new Master silently at a distance. Jesus does not seem to notice it until the moment when He turns around and questions them. [2] Now and then I have had to walk behind Jesus without His speaking to me, without His letting me see His face. It is enough to know that Jesus is there, quite near. Whenever He wishes, He will turn towards me.

When we question Jesus, often instead of answering us He asks us a question. This is how He proceeded with the Doctors of Israel. We are instinctively afraid of the Saviour's questions. But it is by welcoming, loving these questions asked by Jesus that already we hear His answer.

[1] Jn 21, 22.
[2] Jn 1, 38.

The authority with which Jesus speaks is unique. The Jews were struck by His doctrine, because He spoke "as one having power."[1] We hear this tone of authority both when Jesus speaks to us in the privacy of our souls and when we hear the Gospel accounts. Here there is a powerful motive for believing in the Master's word. Who then can speak in such a way? What man would dare to demand this unconditional submission?

There are words and *the* word. "The words which Thou gavest me, I have given to them,"[2] Jesus says to His Father after the Last Supper. Elsewhere He mentions "the word" of the Father.[3] The words: not the complete message, in its unity, but detached words, applicable to special occasions. Among the great number of words which ring in my ears — like so many small coins of no apparent value — there is one intended especially for me: one word (*the* "word") which it is important for me to be able to recognize as uttered for me. This I can achieve only by being attentive to each and every word.

[1] Mt 7, 29.
[2] Jn 17, 8.
[3] Jn 14, 24.

✣ *XIV*

Jesus eludes those who want to make Him king. He is unwilling to give His opinion about the conflicts between Israel and Cæsar.[1] He refuses to help a man who asks Him this, in a disagreement about inheritance. He who has come to cut the roots by which these things hold us captive, would not encourage us in our search for them. " One thing is necessary." Mary left all things in order to listen to the word : she has chosen " the best part."[2]

And yet the word can be expressed in every earthly question provided that it is the

[1] Mt 22, 18.
[2] Lk 10, 42.

Saviour's word which we look for in it. In this way human questions are transformed in Christ.

Let us consider Martha and Mary. Jesus does not blame Martha for attending to domestic cares. What He reproaches her for is for being " careful " and " troubled " about " many things. "[1] She allows herself to be distracted from hearing the word. But it is possible, in the midst of inevitable daily preoccupations, even while serving, to sit down, as it were, at the Lord's feet and listen to Him. The most intense activity does not exclude a glance in the Saviour's direction, cast directly on Jesus. If Martha had realized it, she would have — without stopping to serve — chosen the best part — no less than Mary had done.

The inhabitants of Sichem say to the Samaritan woman : " We now believe, not for thy saying; for we ourselves have heard Him. "[2] A moment is bound to come when the word, which Jesus has interpreted for us and which has directed us towards Him, becomes so authoritative that we are bound to believe by virtue of an immediate experience,

[1] Lk 10, 41.
[2] Jn 4, 42.

of a personal contact. We no longer want only to hear about Him, but to hear Him speak to us.

Man, says Jesus, " *doth live* in every word that proceedeth from the mouth of God. "[1] There is a great difference between tasting from time to time the divine Word and living by it, making it our daily, necessary, essential food.

And Jesus says that of each and every divine word. Whatever be the divine word which we encounter, as strange as it may seem to our present needs, it is for us, provided we know how to make it more intense, a source and power of life.

---

[1] Mt 4, 4.

✣ *XV*

My child, I have so many things to tell you! I would like so much to speak with you, to reveal Myself to you! If only you would turn towards Me, be silent and listen to Me! But you give Me so few opportunities to open My heart to you! Do you want to converse with Me? Even if it were only for a few minutes each day?

When we listen to Jesus, we become accustomed very quickly to His voice. We become capable of perceiving, if I may venture to say so, the Saviour's tone, the style which is peculiar to Him. It is one of simplicity, serene clarity. An authentic word from the Saviour does not sound the same as the echoes of our subconscious or the advances of the enemy. And in each of these words, we sense a firm resting place, something final which puts an end to uncertainties and debates.

" My sheep hear My voice... "[1] By listening to Jesus, by becoming familiar with His voice, we discover in the Master a shepherd and we become His sheep. The relationship between the shepherd and the sheep opens a phase other than the relationship between the disciple and the Master. The shepherd feeds his sheep; he shelters it; he carries it on his shoulders. There is a tenderness appropriate to this relationship.

" I am the good shepherd... "[2] — in the original Greek, the " beautiful " shepherd. This expression is a hellenism; the beautiful and the good are inseparable. The goodness of the shepherd is not only interior; it is a goodness noticed also outwardly. It radiates and attracts. In this way does it share in beauty. In primitive Christian art, the good shepherd is graceful; he has the charm of adolescence. There is in these images a springlike poetry because the Saviour's youth is always new.

[1] Jn 10, 27.
[2] Jn 10, 14.

The shepherd " calleth His own sheep by name and leadeth them out. "[1] Before fulfilling His pastoral office, before leading His flock, Jesus proceeds to a personal recognition of each sheep. The personal relationship has a kind of primacy over the ministry.

" I am the door of the sheep... "[2] Jesus does not say : " I am the door of the sheepfold. " Here again the accent is put on the personal relationship.

" By Me, if any man enter in... "[3] We must therefore pass through this door. We must in some way pass through Jesus Christ. He is at one and the same time the immense door and the " narrow gate. "[4] To pass through Him, we must conform to His dimensions. We must increase and expand, we must humble ourselves and confine ourselves to Christ's standard.

To confine ourselves, yes, certainly. But why increase? Because this door is so big, so high, that he who does not increase, who does not lift up his gaze, who does not ascend, cannot see, cannot find such a door.

[1] Jn 10, 3.
[2] Jn 10, 7.
[3] Jn 10, 9.
[4] Mt 7, 14.

What will he, who has gone through the door and passed through Christ, find? First of all, security: "he shall be saved..."; then freedom, the free usufruct of the world created by God: "he shall go in and go out..."; and finally, the necessary nourishment: "he shall find pastures..."[1]

Immediately after stating that He is the good shepherd, Jesus says: "The good shepherd giveth His life for His sheep."[2] By that He does not add a new characteristic to the notion of good shepherd, but he makes more explicit something which was already included in that notion. What He is really saying is not: "I am the good shepherd, and furthermore, I give My life for My sheep," but rather "I am the good shepherd and *because* I am the good shepherd, I give My life for My sheep." The sacrifice of His own life is contained in the definition of good shepherd. The pastoral and sacrificial theme are really one — completely inseparable one from the other. Generosity (even unto death) is a part of the goodness and beauty of the shepherd. In this pastoral imagery there is much more than a graceful idyll or figure. The Passion of Christ is stamped in it as a watermark in paper.

[1] Jn 10, 9.   [2] Jn 10, 11.

XVI

There are those who refuse to follow Jesus; such was the young man who "became sorrowful, for he was very rich."[1] What became of this young man? We would like to think that later he came back to Jesus, giving everything. We are permitted to cling to such a hope by the very fact that when going away, he "became sorrowful." Not incensed or bitter, but sorrowful. Therefore he was repenting of it.... Grief bears fertile seeds. If I refuse, at least let me be sad about it!

"Sell all whatever thou hast..."[2] Here we see the Saviour's inflexibility in what He demanded of this young man. The heart of

[1] Lk 18, 23.
[2] Lk 18, 22.

Jesus is liquid and burning like molten gold. But His will is as hard as a diamond. In Jesus, there is all the sweetness of the hills of Galilee, but also the severity and clear sharpness of the burnt mountains of Judea.

The shepherd goes in search of his sheep. The Saviour's methods of approach are illustrated by the episode of the Samaritan woman. Jesus goes from Judea into Galilee : " He was of necessity to pass through Samaria, "[1] says the Gospel. It was not the only route possible : Jesus could have followed the other bank of the Jordan. But Jesus must pass near Sichar in order to meet the Samaritan woman there. These are the *musts* of grace, this is the thoughtfulness of Jesus. Is my life woven with such thoughtfulness?

Jesus wants to meet the Samaritan woman near that section of land which Jacob had bequeathed to Joseph. The Samaritans were especially devoted to these two patriarchs. Jesus wants to meet people on their own land, in a place where each soul feels at home.

Jesus " loved Martha and her sister Mary and Lazarus. "[2] The Gospel does not tell us that Jesus loved as a whole the members of

[1] Jn 4, 4.
[2] Jn 11, 5.

the family of Bethany. He loved each one of the three with a special love, with a shade of difference which is not transferable. It is not necessarily a question of a difference of degree, but certainly of that shade of difference...

Jesus asks the Samaritan woman for something to drink.[1] It is He who can give this woman everything, but He puts Himself under obligation to Her. He establishes Himself as a humble person from the outset of the dialogue. Because He thus gives to the Samaritan woman a claim upon Himself it will become easier for Him to establish a claim upon her. The favor which He asked for humbly, opens the door.

It is in a leper's house and in a town named Bethany, which means house of the poor, that Jesus receives on His head, like a royal anointing, the precious perfume which a woman brought in an alabaster jar.[2] Here we have a contrast between abasement and glory, two pivotal points in the Saviour's life. It is in my leprous soul that I shall break at His feet the alabaster jar in which I put my spikenard — the genuine nard (pistikos) of my sorrow and obedience.

[1] Jn 4, 7.
[2] Mk 14, 3.

I am going back in spirit to Jacob's well. Is Jesus very different there from what He is at Bethany? He appears to be the same there, displaying the same calm sympathy, the same simple authority.

Jesus having grown tired sits down on the curb of the well. He is waiting for the Samaritan woman. He is waiting for me. *Quaerens me sedisti lassus...* sings the old mediæval Latin prose. My Saviour, You have grown tired in Your search of me and You have sat down. You did not give up owing to the length of the road or because of the roughness of the road. And now You are seated in that place where You know I am going to pass by for You want me to encounter Your weariness at the same time as Your tenderness — that weariness which explains that affection.

✣ XVII

With a simple phrase, Jesus cures the paralytic who could not go down into the pool at Bethsaida when the angel stirred up its waters.[1] What happened at Bethsaida, at the time of the angel's coming, represents the regular dispensation — and in some way the official one — of grace. But Jesus does not cease to draw near to men and to cure directly and immediately those who cannot plunge into the waters of Bethsaida. That does not mean that we must ignore or despise Bethsaida. But Jesus is bound by nothing. To Him all is possible, without any previous conditions.

[1] Jn 5, 8.

"But I am in the midst of you, as He that serveth." [1] I shall not attain Jesus, if I seek Him reigning in the place of honor. I have to look for Him and find Him in that place where He is hiding, in the last place, in His suffering and humiliated members. It is because they are not looking for Him there that so many men cannot believe in Him or have only a nominal faith in Him. Zacheus has to come down from his sycamore in order to join Jesus in the crowd. [2]

In order to meet her at Jacob's well, Jesus chooses the hour when He knows that the Samaritan woman comes to draw her water each day. It is in our daily needs — in our daily labor — that Jesus wants to meet us.

The blind man whom Jesus had cured noticed, first of all, men "as it were trees walking." [3] When Jesus touched him again, he "saw all things clearly." [4] As long as Jesus has not touched our eyes, we too see other men only vaguely, darkly; our selfishness puts a veil between them and us. It is only after being touched by Jesus that we notice the reality of each being and what is unique about it.

[1] Lk 22, 27.
[2] Lk 19, 6.
[3] Mk 8, 24.
[4] Mk 8, 25.

This new sense of vision improves with the Saviour's repeated touches.

Let us consider the washing of feet on the evening of the Last Supper.[1] The fourth Gospel notes carefully each detail of this episode. We see Jesus get up, take off His tunic, gird Himself with a linen cloth, pour water into a basin, wash the disciples' feet, and finally dry them. Jesus serves, and He serves in the most perfect way possible. Not a thing which is required is omitted. Attention is not only due but is also given to the minutest details.

Mary of Magdala loved Jesus even more it seems than the disciples themselves loved Him. Jesus had driven from her seven devils.[2] The Saviour takes possession of the souls of those who love Him and He does so with all His might, because these souls were once able to open their hearts to more hostile influences. O souls whom the devils have possessed, take courage!

If, among the Saviour's words, I had to choose one of them, only one, which could sum up for unbelievers all the good news, I would

[1] Jn 13, 4.
[2] Lk 8, 2.

choose without hesitation these words : " come to Me all you who labor and are burdened and I will refresh you. "[1] Would you call this simply humanism? No, because it is a question of seeing who dares to speak in such a way.

This text really says everything. It is a call directed at all the suffering in the world, at all those whom evil weighs down. This is the proclamation of a person — Christ — that He is Himself the remedy. The only remedy for men's suffering. Would a man who is only a man say these things? These are the gifts of the liberator to those who come to Him: comfort, consolation, rest. All the truths of divine revelation are not explicitly formulated in these words but all of them are found there implicitly, in germ.

My Saviour, I see the vast suffering mass of people, crushed to the ground; I see this mass stretch forth its arms towards You, crawl along, get up, try to go on towards You, groping, tottering. You are drawing them without their knowing You. In You they have a foreboding of the one who cures, who consoles, who pardons.

[1] Mt 11, 28.

XVIII

" The sower went forth to sow. "[1] Thus begins the parable of the sowing. I have seen Jesus sow for centuries, across the ages. I see Him moving forward, again today, scattering the grain which sometimes falls among thorns, sometimes along the road, sometimes in rocky places and sometimes on good ground. Jesus sows broadcast, He sows even in the midst of the ruins of war and massacres, He will never stop sowing until the end of the world.

Either I can hoard — or I can sow. I must hoard like a miser or sow with Jesus. O Lord,

[1] Mt 13, 3.

everything I accumulate without You is useless. Everything I sow without You is dispersed and remains unfruitful. O Lord teach me to sow along with You.

My child, remember that the sower *went out* to sow. I pass by in front of you, scattering My seed. Do you really want to join Me, to sow together with Me? Begin by leaving your house, by exposing yourself to bad weather and insecurity outside. But to go out of your house is not enough. Go out of yourself.

My child, I am both the sower and the seed. You cannot sow with Me if you do not already possess the seed. You cannot join the sower if you have not already received him as a seed in your soul. The seed must grow within you. The sower must increase within you until he has filled all your being and has outgrown you. Then you will come and sow along with Me.

✠ XIX

Jesus does not promise happiness itself or its various forms. He announces and proclaims the beatitudes.[1] In Hebrew as in Greek the word implies an idea of divine blessing, of supernatural joy. Such is the joy which Jesus communicates: joy which He promised to the poor, to the meek, to the pure, to the afflicted. It is a joy which is just the opposite of men's usual joy; it is a joy based on the reversal of all customary values. The beatitudes are placed on a plane which transcends man. In relation to us, this is something completely different; it has to be

[1] Mt 5, 3.

sought after and explored as something absolutely new.

These beatitudes are within our reach. Is there any joy more visible, more radiant, than the calm joy of those who possess Jesus?

"...In order that My joy may be in you and that your joy may be full."[1] *My* joy, *your* joy : between these two joys there is an important difference. The Saviour's joy, identical with the divine life, is absolute : it exists always and completely; it is not susceptible to increase (at least as far as the divine nature of Jesus is concerned; it is not the same with His human nature). The disciples' joy, however, is expected to increase, to progress, so that it becomes perfect.

Is it accurate to say simply that Jesus *speaks*? It would be more correct to say that, when He speaks, Jesus shows Himself. His words go beyond words. Each one of them reveals the supreme and beloved person. More than receiving merely the words of the beloved, the lover, when he receives the loved one's words, receives the loved one Himself.

[1] Jn 16, 22 ff.

XX

"Jesus wept."[1] The perfect joy of His divine nature did not exclude tears from His human nature. The evangelist adds other touches to his reference to the Saviour's tears. Near Lazarus' tomb the Saviour "groaned,... troubled Himself."[2] How are we to understand this emotion of Christ, because in the end Jesus knows that He is going to raise Lazarus? Perhaps we must see in the Saviour's sorrow something more than compassion for a friend who has died, but who will soon rise again. Jesus weeps over the universal destiny of men, over death which

[1] Jn 11, 35.
[2] Jn 11, 33.

afflicts this human nature of ours which the Father had made so beautiful. Jesus weeps over all of man's suffering, the consequence of sin. The God-Man takes this suffering on Himself. His sorrow is His share in the world's sorrow.

"Dost thou see this woman?," [1] Jesus said to Simon the Pharisee, while the sinful woman washed the Saviour's feet with her tears. Jesus asks me the same question: "Do you see this woman? Have you kissed My feet? Have you washed them with your tears?"

Peter "wept bitterly" [2] when Jesus, leaving Caiphas' house, turned around and looked at the apostle who had denied Him.

Lord Jesus, I should like to weep at your feet. But I have no tears. My eyes are dry and so is my heart. It has become difficult for me to weep. Too many years have passed. Where are the tears of my youth? Lord, they were not for You. But give me this day the ability to weep because of You with my youthful tears. Strike the rock, and make the salty, living spring of tears burst forth. Baptize me in the humility of worthwhile tears.

[1] Lk 7, 44.
[2] Mt 26, 75.

"Woe to you that laugh!"[1] Several times the Gospel shows us Jesus weeping. But never does it mention any laughter from Jesus. Vulgar, heavy, rousing, sarcastic laughter: how incompatible with the picture which the Gospel paints of our Saviour! Jesus never says to His followers: "Laugh." But He does tell them: "Be glad and rejoice"[2] — and this He tells them right before persecution itself. We must rejoice and exult: this emotion which causes lively joy communicated by Jesus is of another order than laughter.

But it would be inconceivable that Jesus did not smile at little children whom He allowed to come to Him; inconceivable, too, that Jesus did not have a friendly, winning smile. When Jesus said to the Syrophenician woman that it is not fair to take bread from children and cast it to dogs,[3] do we not see the smile with which Jesus would have accompanied this so apparently harsh word? But without such a smile, would the woman have dared to use this comparison and evoke the picture of little dogs under the table eating the crumbs which the children allowed to fall?

[1] Lk 6, 25. [2] Mt 5, 12.
[3] Mk 7, 27.

Perhaps Jesus' tears and His smile were very close to one another. Perhaps sometimes they would blend, for the lips can smile when the eyes are still bathed in tears, like a rainbow which begins to shine in the midst of the rain, or the sun's caress on the damp wheat.

✣ *XXI*

Before teaching His disciples the words of the Lord's prayer, Jesus says to them: " Thus therefore shall you pray. "[1] The word " thus " refers not only to the text of the Lord's prayer but also to the way in which it is said. We are certainly meant to pray with the Saviour's words, but especially to pray — as much as a sinful creature is able — as Jesus does, with His dispositions, by entering into His spirit.

Especially at Calvary, during Christ's last agony on the cross we see how He prays. Jesus

[1] Mt 6, 9.

cries out these words: " Father into Thy hands I commend My spirit. " [1]

Only those who have felt crushed at certain times, seeing no way out, and who have found refuge in this supreme act of confidence can understand this cry.

What I should like is to be lifted up, to be held by You, to be carried by You, my Master. By repeating these words " Into Thy hands... " I should like, if I may venture to say so, to remain stubbornly attached to You, hanging on to you, fastened to You, clinging to You. It is at such a time that one experiences what prayer can be.

Jesus shouted His last prayer " with a loud voice, " a voice which muffled all tumults, those without and those within; a voice which expressed the supreme and completely unsurpassable effort. All the powers of being were realized in that shout.

I want to feel in my prayer, through my prayer, that I have no being, that I cannot be and that my being is " in Thy hands. "

Jesus warns His disciples against multiplicity of empty words in prayer. [2] There

[1] Lk 23, 46.
[2] Mt 6, 7.

are times in our life when a need for simplification and unification takes hold of us in such a way that even the perfect prayer, which the Master taught to His disciples, seems too long for us. We need to express our prayer in a single word. This word has been given to us. Jesus! Jesus! It must be said again — not mechanically, but in spirit and in truth.

All the mysteries of our salvation are summed up in the name of Jesus. If we repeat this name, the actuality of Jesus can sink into us, fill us up, saturate us, in such a way that the Word becomes flesh in us. This is not the Incarnation in the literal sense of the word, but a sharing in it through grace.

The name of Jesus penetrates the soul, as a spot of oil spreads silently in all directions.

The Saviour's name contains the world like the colors of the prism which blend into the ray of light. In the Word the Father has created all things.

Invoke the name of Jesus on everything which exists and the world will be transfigured, christified, and given its true meaning.

You, Lord Jesus, pray in me. Let me be silent so that Your voice alone may be heard. If Your prayer becomes mine, if I let You pray in me then all events and all creatures in the world will enter into my prayer and will be influenced by it.

Let us consider Jesus and Creation. The intimate relationship which exists between Jesus and creation concerns not only men, for it is not only in His word that God created the universe, but the incarnate God draws towards Himself all words. As St. Paul said: The whole of creation " subject to vanity, "[1] to physical evil, to catastrophes, to the severity of natural laws, " groaneth and travaileth in pain, even till now "[2] and " the expectation of the creature waiteth for the revelation of the sons of God. "[3]

---

[1] Rom 8, 20. [2] Rom 8, 22.
[3] Rom 8, 19.

✠ *XXII*

Let us consider Jesus and nature. That passage of the Gospel in which Jesus evokes the lilies of the field — whose adornment outshines Solomon's glory [1] — is frequently quoted. Here Jesus invites us to admire the beauty of the divine work. More than that, He exhorts us to have faith in the Father who, if He thus clothes the transient grass, will all the more clothe His children. But here we have only one aspect, and perhaps not the most profound one, of the relationship between Jesus and the natural world.

A symbolic interpretation of nature does not exhaust the meaning of nature. It is true

[1] Mt 6, 29.

that nature is an open book in which each detail suggests in veiled terms the realities of the supernatural life. It is a stroke of mediæval genius that such a strong intuition of symbols existed. But there is more than symbolism here.

Nature is oriented. It reveals an ordered effort towards Jesus Christ. Jesus is the direction and terminus of all evolution, the secret cause, the compass needle and vector — as physicists would say — of natural phenomena.

" If these shall hold their peace, the stones will cry out, "[1] Jesus said to the Pharisees who wanted to find fault with the disciples. Jesus is alluding to what is the proper function of nature which is noticed only by the believer. Nature murmurs the Saviour's name. Even if original sin has inflicted painful deviations on it, it cries out in the Saviour's direction.[2] All the elements tend towards the God-Man. Stone and rock will furnish the Saviour's sepulchre. Water will attain its highest end in regenerating Baptism. Olive trees will produce oil which anoints and cures the sick

[1] Lk 19, 40.
[2] Rom 8, 22.

in the name of Jesus. Grains of wheat and grapes from the vine will produce that bread and wine from which the Master will bring about the mystery of His broken body and of the blood which He will shed. From the tree will be formed the wood of the cross. In this way one and the same impulse will transport all nature towards Christ, and with it, all human labor, — that of harvesters, bakers, vinegrowers and others — who help in this elevation, in this transfiguration.

✥ *XXIII*

Jesus is the desired one, or rather He is desire itself. He is not only the desire of souls, but the desire of all creation.

Let us consider Jesus in the wilderness "with beasts."[1] This brief reference in the Gospel opens certain perspectives to pious meditation. Wouldn't the animal creation be touched, in a way which we do not know, by the Saviour's nearness and grace?

"Not a sparrow," said Jesus "is forgotten before God."[2] In that statement consists the dignity, the value of the animal world. Each

[1] Mk 1, 13.
[2] Cfr. Mt 10, 29.

animal pre-exists in God's *thought;* it has been loved by God; even before its birth, it has been the object of God's intention and loving care.

Let us consider Jesus in the house. " Zacheus... this day I must abide in thy house. "[1] Christ has a relationship with all creation, but it is first of all in our house that He wishes to be known by us. It is in our family circle that we must first of all explore and then allow the Saviour's person to shine forth.

Jesus sends some of His followers to preach the Kingdom of God in far-off cities. [2] To others, He says : " Go into thy house to thy friends, and tell them how great things the Lord hath done for thee and hath had mercy on thee. "[3] No one who has met Jesus is dispensed from speaking out in favour of Him. The testimony which we give in our own house, in our natural milieu, is perhaps more difficult than the testimony of the wandering apostle. It entails a great deal of courage and humility. But it does not entail a great many words. This domestic testimony can even be rendered in absolute silence. What is essential is that we be " changed " and that our change, by the

[1] Lk 19, 5.   [2] Lk 10, 1.
[3] Mk 5, 19.

mental considerations which it provokes, be capable of changing other men.

Jesus says to the paralytic: " Take up thy bed, and go into thy house. "[1] This bed will act as a witness. It will recall the infirmity of which the man has been cured. Jesus does not want us to forget or ignore what we have been saved from, what has been forgiven. The paralytic's bed is a sign. It will help to confess Jesus. Those of us who know that we have been changed must realize what the Saviour has worked in us.

[1] Mt 9, 6.

✠ *XXIV*

"Lovest thou Me?"[1] The question which Jesus asked Simon Peter is still being asked of each one of us. It is the essential question. My answer to this question defines my relationship with the Saviour.

Do I dare to say with Peter : " Lord, Thou knowest all things, Thou knowest that I love Thee."[2] But alas how often it happens that my life and deeds contradict such a statement!

Shall I humbly admit that I do not have this love? Shall I say with simplicity, perhaps truthfully : " No, Lord, I do not love Thee?"

[1] Jn 21, 15.
[2] Jn 21, 17.

This radical denial does not quite produce the right sound. For even in my worst failings the memory and image of the Saviour are never completely erased from my mind, do not cease to attract me. What a complex situation for the sinner who, from the depths of his misery, and without having the strength to break his bonds, yet turns his head towards Him with whom he longs to be united.

The only answer which I can give is: " Lord, You know all things, You know that I want to love You; give me Your love. "

Jesus entrusts to Peter the care of feeding His lambs and sheep, because Peter loves more " than these. "[1] All authority, all responsibility in the Church must express a very great love. The shepherd according to Christ's heart is consecrated to charity. The washing of feet before the Last Supper is the fundamental mystery of the apostolic state.

Jesus asks Peter: " Lovest Thou Me? "[2] But every faithful member also has the right to ask the shepherd set over the flock: " Do you love me? Do you love me more than these, more than my relatives love me, more than those of this world who love me with a natural

[1] Jn 21, 15.
[2] Jn 21, 17.

love? How have you tried to communicate to me the supernatural love of the one who has sent you? When have you washed my feet?"

That frightening statement: "If you love Me, keep My commandments,"[1] condemns me. To keep the Saviour's word means to observe His commandments. The most obvious meaning of the phrase is this: the sign of genuine love for Jesus is a life in conformity with His precepts.

Another meaning which does not exclude the first is: only the one who loves Jesus can keep His word. It is a love which precedes obedience as a condition for obedience. If obedience preserves love, if it gives it continuity and security, it derives from love its origin, its end, its internal power.

O Master, how can I obey You if I do not love You? First of all convert me to Your love, then I shall know how to obey You. I am so full of human frailty that I cannot keep Your word if I am not sustained by Your love. If my heart is not full of love, temptation will take its place. Fill up my heart as one fills a glass of water to the brim, but exclude all impurities

---

[1] Jn 14, 15.

from it. Only the hope of gaining Your love prevents me from being discouraged about eventually abiding by Your word.

It is this complete filling up of the heart which expresses the great commandment: " Thou shalt love the Lord thy God with thy whole heart and with thy whole soul and with thy whole mind. Thou shalt love thy neighbour as thyself. "[1] If it is filled up, it will lead us to a thorough examination of conscience: is there room in me, even at this moment, for anything other than the love of Christ?

Was much forgiven the sinful woman *because* she loved much?[2] Or has she loved much because much has been forgiven her? The Greek text of Christ's statement admits of both interpretations. Both express a profound truth. The first makes pardon a reply to love. It goes without saying that we reject the meaning which degrades the word " love " and allows it to cover all possibilities. Even in the first interpretation love, which calls for pardon, is already a grace coming from the Saviour's initiative. In the second interpretation, where pardon engenders love, the Saviour's initiative

[1] Mt 22, 37 ff.
[2] Lk 7, 47.

remains equally sovereign; it provokes the first movement of repentance without which there could be no forgiveness, then forgiveness itself which ratifies this repentance, and finally love, which is the forgiven soul's response. If I loved Jesus to the extent to which He has forgiven me, would I not be afire with love?

" Abide in My love. "[1] The Greek text makes it clear that it is not a question of our love for Jesus but of the love which Jesus Himself possesses. " Abide in the love which is Mine, in the love which animates Me, in the love which expresses My whole nature. " But the love which is in Jesus is the source and efficacy of our love for Him.

---

[1] Jn 15, 9.

✣ *XXV*

It is not enough to know Jesus as the Master who speaks to me and the friend who attracts me. The good shepherd is also the Lamb of God. He is the victim who has offered Himself for me in sacrifice. Without an intimate knowledge of the lamb, I cannot know the heart of Christ.

John the precursor proclaimed Jesus as the Lamb of God.[1] This proclamation is the first episode in the Saviour's public life after His baptism. It is this proclamation which led John's two disciples to follow Jesus in silence. The revelation of the lamb is the threshold of the mystery of salvation.

[1] Jn 1, 29.

The precursor made one true discovery of the lamb, or rather, the revelation of the Messias as lamb was made to John. " And I knew Him not, "[1] said John. The precursor had spoken of the axe lain at the root of the trees. He had announced One mightier than himself[2] who, with the winnowing fan in His hand, will cleanse the air and burn the straw.[3] But he had said nothing of the lamb. Now he proclaims the lamb, that lamb who forms a contrast with the formidable winnower. John's revelation is unexpected. As soon as he sees Jesus coming, the day after His baptism, this cry : " Behold the Lamb of God, "[4] comes not only from John's lips but also from his heart.

The next day, two days after the baptism, John repeats the proclamation : " Behold the Lamb of God. " This time Jesus does not come towards John, but He goes towards His ultimate destiny. Such are the two circumstances in which he who discovers the lamb gives witness of Him (and in so few words). The first instance is when the lamb comes towards us, the second is when He goes towards others.

[1] Jn 1, 31.
[2] Cfr. Mk 1, 7.
[3] Cfr. Mt 3, 12.
[4] Jn 1, 29.

" Behold the Lamb of God. "[1] Here is the Lamb, concentrate your attention on Him.

John the Baptist, who invites us to look at the lamb, to become aware of His presence, pronounces these words while looking at Jesus. The Greek word used by the Evangelist describes a prolonged, penetrating look.

Have I looked at Jesus only with a passing glance, or have I put into that look something of that calm insistence and depth which John put into his?

Jesus is the Lamb of God. He is not the lamb chosen by men, but the lamb which God Himself furnishes for the sacrifice. He is the lamb which has always belonged to God and will belong to Him forever. He is the only lamb worthy of God, perfect and spotless. He is the real and definitive paschal lamb, the only one whose immolation brings with it salvation.

The lamb is the little one of the flock. Littleness is an essential element of the concept of the Lamb of God. It is in this way that the notion of lamb unites with the notion of childhood.

---

[1] Jn 1, 29.

THE WISDOM OF GOD

✜ *XXVI*

The sign by which the shepherds will recognize the Saviour is that they will find "the infant wrapped in swaddling clothes and laid in a manger."[1] No sign of power accompanies the birth of Jesus Christ. On the contrary, God become man will make Himself known first of all by His poverty, His humility, His weakness. As a small child wrapped in swaddling clothes, He is at the mercy of those who press round Him. He depends on them. He cannot resist anyone. He is unable to exercise His will, nor can He defend Himself. As He appears in His birth,

[1] Lk 2, 12.

so will He appear in His passion, and that is how He wants me to be.

Jesus calls to Him the little children: " Suffer the little children to come unto Me... for of such is the Kingdom of God. "[1] He takes a little child and places it near Him: " Whosoever shall not receive the Kingdom of God as a little child, shall not enter into it. "[2]

The adult disciple of Christ does not have to strip himself of the human qualities which a child does not yet possess. But he does have to strip himself of his adult faults and assume all the positive qualities of a little child.

In Christ's eyes the soul's ascent towards God is also a descent. It consists especially in making oneself small. " He that is the lesser among you all, he is the greater. "[3] In the Church of the child of Bethlehem, in the Church of the lamb, there exists an invisible hierarchy of humility.

Jesus prefers the poor and simple means — those which the child itself makes use of. He could have had manna sent down from Heaven, but it is with a young boy's five

[1] Mk 10, 14. [2] Mk 10, 15.
[3] Lk 9, 48.

barley loaves and two little fishes that He feeds the multitudes in the desert.[1] And yet these loaves and fishes must be brought to Jesus; He must give thanks over them, and distribute them with His own hand to the disciples. Simple means — the child's poor provisions — will be efficacious, if they are blessed by Jesus.

In His discourse after the Last Supper, Jesus calls His disciples " little children."[2] Not just " children " but " little children. " The word implies both the notion of kinship and of deep affection, and also the notion of a particular solicitude towards individuals who are not yet mature. Master, You who called Your disciples " little children, " I remind You that I have not the perfection, nor the strength of Your maturity as Son of God. Grant that I may remain, or rather, become, a little child in Your hands. Grant that I may be led. For the sin of the first man was that of no longer wanting to be led, hand in hand, by the Father in Heaven. I have the weakness of childhood; grant me the docility and complete confidence of a small child.

[1] Mt 14, 19.
[2] Jn 13, 33.

For whoever follows the lamb's little way, the way of childhood begun at Bethlehem — for him all that is small becomes great.

The lamb is a symbol of simplicity, innocence and purity. "If I wash thee not, thou shalt have no part with Me,"[1] Jesus says to Peter. I can have a part with Jesus only if I am pure. But He alone can make me pure.

---

[1] Jn 13, 8.

XXVII

"Now you are clean, by reason of the word which I have spoken to you."[1] The Saviour's word is not only an incitement to purification and an instrument through which this purification is declared, but it also purifies in a substantial way. If we receive this word by opening our heart to it, by letting ourselves be possessed by it, we are made clean even before forgiveness has been formally asked for and granted. For we receive the Word made flesh. This purification lasts as long as the union of the soul with the Word lasts.

[1] Jn 15, 3.

At the time of the wedding feast of Cana, Jesus orders the servants to fill with water the six stone water-jars [1] which were used for legal ceremonial washings. It is this water which will be changed into wine. Water purifies. Wine brings strength and joy. It expresses the Saviour's delight in those whose guest He is. But before the water becomes wine the ceremoniel water-jars must be filled " up to the brim. " [2]

Charity according to Christ cannot exist wherever there is no purity. It is only in the soul which has become a water-jar filled up to the brim with the water of purity that this water can be changed into the wine of charity.

Master, how am I supposed to understand your parable of the wedding feast? The king had cast into outer darkness the man who did not have on a wedding garment. [3] But this man was not one of the expected guests. He was one of those whom the servants went to seek in the highways and byways. He could not have put on a wedding garment.

My child, no one has a wedding garment before going into the house. It is in the house

[1] Cfr. Jn 2, 7.   [2] Jn 2, 7.
[3] Mt 22, 13.

that one can get one. You must ask Me for one. I give wedding garments to all those whom I invite to the wedding feast. Without Me, you have nothing, you can do nothing. It is from Me that you have to expect everything.

The notions of purification and wedding garment arouse in me an awareness of sin, because the vision of the lamb is also the vision of my sin.

"Behold the Lamb of God, behold Him who taketh away the sin of the world."[1] The discovery of the lamb implies our awareness of sin, of injury, of an unbearable burden.

Not only does the Lamb of God take away the weight of sin from our shoulders, but He takes it on His own shoulders. He carries it off, bears it.

The sin of the world is not simply the sum total of the sins of men. It is the expression of the original corruption common to all humanity.

This corruption and this sin of the world become actualized in my personal sins.

---

[1] Jn 1, 29.

✣   *XXVIII*

" Go, call thy husband... " [1] Jesus was about to reveal to the Samaritan woman the mystery of living water. But at this point He interrupts His discourse rather abruptly and calls upon the Samaritan woman to reveal the evil of her life. The Samaritan woman restricts herself to a stammering half confession. Jesus is more explicit about things. He puts His finger on the wound and incises it: the succession of five husbands, the present state of concubinage....

Jesus does not let His dialogue with us go on for a long time without confronting us with

[1] Jn 4, 16.

the immediate realities of our life. He asks us about our secret wounds. Perhaps we would prefer to stay on the level of ideas and listen to Jesus develop a doctrine, a general message. But Jesus cuts us short: " Go, call thy husband.... " [1]

Jesus is so anxious to bring sin out in the open that He says to the paralytic from Capharnaum: " Son, thy sins are forgiven thee " [2] and not " be thou cured! "

Whenever we would perhaps expect Jesus to speak of social reform and material improvements, He speaks to us of sin, repentance, forgiveness. Certainly, a complete attachment to the Gospel implies, necessitates external reforms. But whether it be a question of problems such as sickness, work, oppression and economic justice, sin is there in the background. True liberation is bound up with conversion.

The more I grow in the knowledge of Jesus, the more I see that everything in my life which seems incidental or physically accidental is bound up in some way with sin, original or personal. It is the complete text of

[1] Jn 4, 16.
[2] Mt 9, 2.

my life which I shall read and interpret differently, according as I am convinced or not of the reality and gravity of sin.

Does not the painful failure of certain of today's Christian movements stem from the fact that they never mention sin by calling it sin? This is not the way that Jesus spoke.

✠ *XXIX*

Jesus announces to the Apostles that one of them will betray Him. They do not doubt the Master's word; they do not cry out: " Master, it is impossible! " But they become sad and say one after the other: " Is it I? "[1]

The experience of my own falls should make me very humble. I can never exclude the possibility of a new offense. I should ask " Am I going to betray again? Am I the next traitor? "

" What will you give me, and I will deliver Him unto you? "[2] To Satan I repeat the

[1] Mt 26, 22.
[2] Mt 26, 15.

question which Judas asked the priests: " What pleasure will you give me? If you grant me this or that, I will deliver Him unto you... " Perhaps I mumble this suggestion with my eyes turned away, or perhaps by washing my hands, but not without feeling qualms of conscience. But all the same, I will deliver Him...

Poor soul, you want Me and you also want to betray Me. This is why you want something else instead of Me. You cannot really want Me if you do not want Me alone.

" Jesus he delivered up to their will. "[1] The phrase which the Gospel uses in speaking of Pilate applies to me every time I personally cooperate with the tempter and everytime I cooperate in another's sin.

" Dost thou betray the Son of Man with a kiss?"[2] The kiss by which Judas betrays His Master is every prayer which I venture to say without rooting out from my heart all complacency towards evil.

" This man also was with Him... thou also art one of them. "[3] This thought haunts me, runs through me, whenever in my sin I cannot lose the memory of the time when I, like Peter, followed Jesus.

[1] Lk 23, 25.
[2] Lk 22, 48.
[3] Lk 22, 56 ff.

My Saviour, it is through the secret wounds of my soul, through my sins that You pave Your way towards me.

Jesus, You are present at my sin. When I sin, you are still within me, silent. Your very presence condemns what I do. But at the same time, You understand me and You understand my sin more profoundly than I understand myself or my sin, for You are closer to me than I am to myself. For me You are not an unknown judge. You identify Yourself with the sinner who is before You, and yet You are at that moment the very opposite of what I am. But You embrace me by your immense presence and pity.

Your presence and pity are felt, O Master, during the very act of that sin which I do not have the courage to interrupt; this same presence and pity make it possible for me to utter a cry of disgust, anguish and horror and to appeal to You, to Your name : Jesus!

My Saviour, Your presence at my sin is a great grace. Your hand is stretched out to draw me away from the abyss. But if by committing the sin, I reject that final grace, what will become of me?

You do not pass any formal sentence. Your very person, Master, is the judgment which condemns me, but it is also a proclamation and a pardon. There would be no talk of pardon if there had not been talk of judgment.

My guilty past or present, how guilty they are, belong to the order of grace in so far as all human destiny is linked to the plan of grace willed by God. My personal discords still remain parts of the universal symphony of grace. Yet this consideration cannot justify the discord because it is opposed to grace — and that is death. But the opposition to grace, discord and sin are still potentially in the order of grace as long as my sorrow and Your forgiveness can still intervene. For that, O Saviour, be blessed!

In Christ there is rejection as well as election. United to Christ, I am accepted because of the Beloved and in the Beloved. As a sinner I am rejected in Jesus, since He who did not know sin was made sin for us. A great exchange was accomplished on Golgotha between the sinner and his God. It is I who sin and it is Jesus who dies. Sin has been enclosed in Christ's heart. The God-man Himself becomes the rejected one, the condemned one. For the believer's piety there is still a great deal to explore in this mystery — insofar as any divine mystery can be explored. Master, allow me to speak to You about that.

✠ *XXX*

O Jesus, the mystery of Judas depresses me, or rather — because I do not know what the traitor's last sentiments were — the mystery of all sinners who die without turning to You depresses me. I know that what You said about the separation of the sheep from the goats and of the fire which dieth not cannot be erased from the book. I know that the possibility of certain of His creatures saying " no " to God for eternity, is a terrible but necessary consequence of the liberty which has been given to us. I also know that we have no certainty that any man has been rejected forever. I know all that. And yet... Why did Your Father create that kind of man whom He foresaw would not adhere to Him?

Master, I put my question before you with humility and docility. Teach me.

My child, I could simply tell you: this question is beyond you, wait with confidence for the day when you will know, when you will see. The full light of these divine mysteries is not given to those who are still in this world.

However I shall tell you more. I shall not grant you a personal revelation, but I shall remind you only of what you already know or ought to know.

I have helped you to believe and to understand a little that the mystery of choice takes place in Me. It is in Me that those who love Me are accepted. What I should like to convince you of now is that it is also in Me that the mystery of rejection receives its solution and light.

Every man has the right to hear this word from me: " I am your justice. "[1] And every man has the right to say to me, the just One: " I am your sin. " I have communicated my justice to sinners — if they accept it — and I have borne the weight of rejection due to the sins of all. Just as there is a link between every chosen one and the justice which I have

[1] Cfr. 1 Cor 1, 30.

acquired for him on the cross, so also there is a link between every non-repentant sinner and Myself, in so far as, in his place, I assumed on the cross his sin and his condemnation. Because I took the place of the sinner, even though the sinner spurned the exchange, there was a certain exchange between him and Me. It is in the continuation, in the repercussions of this exchange that you have to meditate on the mystery of rejection.

Listen to Me carefully, My child. I did not say that on the cross I saved those who do not want to assimilate throughout their life the salvation which I offered. I mean only one thing *at this very noment*: a real contact has been established on the cross and remains between Myself and the non-repentant sinner. I have had a full and paramount experience of condemnation. In Me, absolute holiness has been in contact with every sin, with the sin of every sinner. In Me, absolute glory has been in contact with absolute rejection, with the rejection of every sinner.

What were, what are the results of this contact? My child, I shall not tell you now anything more definite. I wish only to show you the horizon without giving you the possibility of measuring it. Believe with all your heart every word of my Gospel concerning the sinner who does not repent. Do not indulge in speculations and discussions on the number of these sinners, on the duration and form of their rejection. Assert what My apostles have asserted, what My Church asserts. Say nothing more.

But be well aware, My child, that you do not yet know the depths of My heart. You will know them later.

Stand in fear of being rejected, My child. Do not trust those who attach little importance to preoccupation with their personal salvation. I have not spoken in this way, but never forget that the good shepherd leaves all his faithful sheep to look for and to bring back on his shoulders the fugitive, lost sheep.

I hope it will be enough for you to be assured of one thing, it is this : I am, and My own person is the answer to your anxious question about the non-repentant sinner.

If my person is the answer, you must catch hold of the meaning of this answer even obscurely. Do not be in a hurry to translate the answer into words. Look, and ponder in silence. The reply can only conform to my person. Contemplate the image of the crucified. He is the answer to this problem, to all problems.

In the solution of the problem which causes you so much agony, some day you will see My sanctity and My justice shining forth. My mercy and love will not be less resplendent. Justice will blaze forth through mercy and mercy through justice. It will then be capable of being as much a joyful mystery as a glorious one. The very mystery of the non-repentant sinner will reveal My love for men but without evil obtaining any impunity or complacency. My apostle told you that I shall be all in all. I cannot tell you now how that will come about. That is the divine secret. Only believe and hope.

Master, I thank You for the peace which Your words give me. I do not seek to go beyond what You tell me. I still do not see the landscape, but I already foresee the light in which it will be bathed. Yet this is what happens to me : the more I cast the light of Your person on the sin of the world, the more the awareness and memory of my own sins weigh me down and sadden me.

I believe in forgiveness asked and received; I believe that You fill up the abyss of the sinner's unworthiness. But what about all those who have suffered at my expense, whom I have injured...?

✢ *XXXI*

My child, you do not yet know what these words mean: "I have made Myself into sin for you."[1] You are thinking with horror of the cruel evil you have committed either recently or many years ago towards this or that person. You know that they have suffered because of you and that to repair this suffering is now impossible. Listen to Me. I have taken the place of those victims of your selfish cruelty. It is no longer against them, it is against Me that your offense is directed. And on the cross I took your place in so far as you were guilty of this offense.

[1] Cfr. 2 Cor 5, 21.

I am the knot tying all these elements together. I alone can untie it, because I have taken on Myself both the damage caused and the cause of the damage, and because in Me dwell expiation and forgiveness. When it is too late to repair the evil as far as the victims are concerned, or even if you can still repair it, cast your sin upon Me, turn it over to Me. Strip yourself of every remnant of personal justification. Through faith take hold of the redemption and salvation which I offer you. Come to Me entirely naked, no longer waiting for anything but My mercy. Stop wondering " How can I repair? " Reparation will come about as a result of your most intimate union with Me. It is by your faith in Me, not by your reparation, that you will be justified. But you cannot open your heart to living faith, to saving faith, to My grace, to My justice unless you are willing to accomplish their works and bear their fruits. I am the One who shall repair, but you shall repair through Me, with Me, and in Me. In order to repair begin by throwing yourself in My arms.

My Saviour, tell me again how You take my sins upon Yourself.

Yes, My child, I want to make you more aware of this mysterious transfer. I should like more men to be aware of it. Many men feel very keenly the heartbreak by which they throw their sins at My feet. Many men also feel very vividly the peace and authority which accompany My word, when it announces, when the Church announces : " Thy sins are forgiven thee." [1] But there are far fewer who know how to perceive the act by which the Lamb of God takes away sin and takes it upon Himself. I have taught you that I am present at your sinning — that my presence is both condemning and compassionate. Then I implore your gaze, your adherence. If you give them to Me, the heart of the act is displaced. It is no longer sin which is at the center. All the evil forces are deflected. It is now I who hold the central position. In this second you are freed. In this second is actualized what happened, when at Gethsemani and on Golgotha I assumed yourself and this sin. The crisis is no longer between you and sin. It is between you and Me. From My heart a ray descends upon you. It draws you, takes hold of you, and your gaze reaches up to Me because you allow your soul to follow the ray....

[1] Mt 9, 2.

✠ *XXXII*

Jesus took aside the twelve and said to them: " Behold, we go up to Jerusalem, and the Son of Man shall be betrayed. "[1]

The Gospel points out very well that this was said in private conversation. It is only to the apostles and not to the disciples that Jesus, on the uphill road, confides the secret of the trip. Certainly Jesus now expects each Christian to take part in the decisive event which took place in Jerusalem. But Jesus remains the Master of time and of individual callings. He chooses the time when He invites

[1] Mt 20, 18.

His disciple to share in the apostles' privilege and go up with Him to Jerusalem, keeping in mind the sad ending.

How many Christians have heeded this invitation? How many have grasped that what happened in Jerusalem, what continues to happen in the eternal, invisible Jerusalem, is what is most important in the world?

Master, I have heard the invitation. You took me aside on the road. You want me to cut myself off from other men in order to be better united with them and to go along with You to the end of Your journey. The meaning and aspect of this journey You reveal to me and will go on revealing to me.

Master, starting today, with the help of Your grace I should like the ascent to Jerusalem and whatever I shall see and hear there about You during that last great week to be the dominant interest of my life. This week must be the norm of all the rest, the circle both small and immense where all the rest will be included and of which You will be the center.

Now I turn my back on everything I have looked for and followed. And now I am sorry for everything in my past life which cannot be a part of the great mystery of Your pasch, and to which You wish me to aspire.

And now I shall climb up to Jerusalem with You. Let all flesh now keep silence.

In the fourth Gospel the account of the last pasch and of the Passion is introduced by these words: " Jesus having loved His own who were in the world, He loved them unto the end. "[1]

" Unto the end " is obvious because not only did Jesus love men until the last moment of His earthly existence, but He loved them completely, entirely, perfectly, definitively. He loved them to the highest possible degree. His Passion adds the finishing touch to His love. There the disciple's probing of Jesus is deepest and most fruitful. There I discover how much and at what a price I am loved. In His immolation the Lamb of God is the lamb to the highest degree and manifests Himself as the lamb. Master, show me the lamb.

---

[1] Jn 13, 1.

✠   *XXXIII*

"With desire I have desired to eat this pasch with you."[1]   It is not a question only of the pasch which preceded the first Good Friday nor of the pasch which we celebrate each year.   Every moment can become a pasch.   A pasch is an intimate meal with Jesus in which we are united to the divine life which is given for the salvation of the world, a union with the broken body and the shed blood.   This special union distinguishes the pasch from union with Christ in a general sense.   The whole paschal mystery, the cross and the resurrection is in the Lord's Supper.

[1] Lk 22, 15.

The mystery of the Last Supper is not limited to the visible participation in the Eucharistic gifts, in the assembly of the faithful. An internal, invisible, purely spiritual Last Supper can take place in my soul at every moment and everywhere. "If any man opens the door to Me, I will come in to him and will sup with him."[1] The invisible Last Supper is no less real than the visible one but it is of another order and to distinguish between these two orders we must have a very deep respect.

"With desire I have desired to eat this pasch with you."[2] To which pasch does he refer? The last one which Jesus will celebrate before His death. The one in which He will reveal to His disciples the mystery of the true paschal lamb. The paschal meals which He longs to eat with me will enable me to discover the lamb.

Jesus puts this question to the Master of the house: "Where is My refectory where I may eat the pasch...?"[3] This question takes on a much richer meaning if we refer to the Greek text of St. Mark: *katalyma mou*, My dwelling, My reception room. In this question

---

[1] Ap 3, 20. [2] Lk 22, 15.
[3] Mk 14, 14.

there is a blending of humility and command. Jesus asks where " His " room is. He demands this with assurance, with the authority of ownership. This room is His, He has engaged it. But He was obliged to borrow it from a man. Jesus begs for my soul in order that He may celebrate His paschal meal there. For my soul belongs to Him. He is willing to come as a guest, He demands my hospitality.

" The Master saith, My time is near at hand, with thee I make the pasch with My disciples. "[1] " With My disciples... " because the Master's pasch is always social. It is never only individual. Even if it is a question of that invisible Last Supper which Jesus can celebrate at any moment in the upper room of my soul, this room must remain open to all of Christ's disciples. If I am with Jesus, I have to be with Peter, Andrew, James, John, Paul and all the apostles, and all those who either in past centuries or today, have been or are the Saviour's disciples. Jesus speaks of His disciples in these terms : " Go, tell My brethren... "[2] I cannot isolate myself from the Saviour's brethren without separating

[1] Mt 26, 18.
[2] Mt 28, 10.

myself from Him. I must commune with them in the same faith, with the same affection.

The phrase which shows us Jesus getting up to wash His disciples' feet begins in this way: " Knowing that the Father had given Him all things into His hands... "[1] The full awareness of divine authority which is invested in Him becomes for Jesus the very basis for an act of humility.

Simon Peter's attitude at the time of the washing of feet[2] clearly indicates the temptations which can assail a sincere disciple. The impulsive Peter exaggerates in two opposite senses. First of all he does not want Jesus to wash him, then he wants Jesus to wash not only his feet, but his head. We would often like to decide what the Master should do and how He should do it. What Jesus desires is that we let ourselves be directed. This is loving submission to His initiatives even though we do not understand them.

If, in imitating Jesus, you kneel to wash another's feet, it is at this point that the towel with which you wiped them will become for you Veronica's towel: on it the Saviour's face will be impressed.

[1] Jn 13, 3.
[2] Jn 13, 8.

Jesus knows that Judas is betraying Him. During the Last Supper He gives him, before the others, " bread dipped. "[1] The episode is disturbing. Is there in it a sign of condemnation or a last appeal of grace? " And after the morsel Satan entered into Judas... "[2] Perhaps we are allowed to think that the external mark of predilection which Judas receives shows again mercy on the part of the Saviour. He is offered one last chance. If we consider carefully the circumstances in which we fall into sin and especially the immediate prelude to our falls, we see that until the last minute the Master multiplies His veiled interventions, His discreet appeals, the descending movements of grace, the touches of secret affection, in order to sustain our weakening will. The history of each of our sins is also the history of a manifestation *in extremis*, as it were, of divine piety. If only we knew, we could read the signs!

---

[1] Jn 13, 26.
[2] Jn 13, 27.

✠   *XXXIV*

The breaking of bread is the central act of Christianity.

At the Last Supper Jesus breaks bread and distributes it.[1] He pours wine and distributes it. It is not enough to say that Jesus gives Himself. He gives Himself as a piece of broken bread and as poured-out wine; He gives His broken body and His shed blood. The Lamb of God is immolated for the life and salvation of the world.

O Jesus, grant me union with You in Your immolation. In Your hands make of my life a libation poured out to God and to men.

[1] Mt 26, 26.

Pour me into Your cup as spilt wine. Make me a piece of bread broken by Your very own hands, held in Your hands, distributed by Your hands. I am willing to be broken by You. Drown my sins and my person in Your blood. Grant that I may die to myself in order to be born to You, to Your brethren! Since I am a member of Your body, offer me to God, and give me to others with Your own body and blood.

Only when the Master broke bread were the eyes of the disciples of Emmaus opened and they recognized Jesus.[1] The presence of Jesus and the breaking of bread are inseparable. Wherever the bread is broken Jesus is there. The Gospel does not specify what the breaking of bread at Emmaus was. Was it a renewal of the mystery of the Last Supper or simply an act of love? Whatever this broken bread may be — whether it be the mystery of the body and blood of Christ communicated to men, or the help brought to those who are hungry, or that friendly sharing of life which a meal symbolizes — this broken bread is the sign by which the Saviour's disciples are recognized. It is a profound

[1] Cfr. Lk 24, 30 f.

and complex sign in its very indetermination. By the breaking of bread performed in the Saviour's spirit, the Saviour's presence is made known.

Jesus is the " bread which cometh down from heaven. "[1] The Gospel also calls it the " bread of life. "[2] There is much more in the notion " bread of life " than in that of " living bread. " To speak of a living bread is to say that life is a quality belonging to this bread. To speak of the bread of life is to state that this quality can be communicated. The bread of life is a food which gives and engenders life.

---

[1] Jn 6, 33.
[2] Jn 6, 35.

✠ *XXXV*

The fourth Gospel places the discourse in which Jesus confines His most profound and intimate teachings after the Last Supper.[1] When I have sat down with Jesus at His supper, when I have been united to the life given for men, the moment will have come for me to listen to certain words, until then reserved, and to receive the supreme confidences of the Friend. Then He will speak to me about Himself.

He cannot speak about Himself without speaking of His Father, for the mystery of Jesus is essentially concerned with this filial relationship. Not to see this is to read the Gospel

[1] Jn 13, 33 ff.

incompletely, to ignore its foundation and its center — rather than to see in it above all the relationship between the Saviour and men. There is first of all the relationship between the Father and His only Son. The Word, says the prologue of the fourth Gospel, is from all eternity " with the Father, "[1] or if we wish to translate the Greek text more exactly, " towards the Father. " Jesus is oriented, turned, in some way drawn towards His Father. His interior life is movement, an impetus towards the Father. This vital impetus explains and exhausts the Saviour's existence and secret. " I live by the Father... " Should this concern us? Let us complete the Gospel quotation : " As I live by the Father, so he that eateth Me, the same also shall live by Me. "[2] Do we know how to see all there is in this " so "? Our intimacy with the Saviour depends on the intimacy between the Father and His Son. On another level it is its effect and reflection.

Jesus summed up this truth but in veiled terms when He said to the Samaritan woman : " If thou didst know the gift of God! "[3] Jesus does not speak here of any particular gift.

[1] Jn 1, 1. [2] Jn 6, 58.
[3] Jn 4, 10.

God's gift is the sum total of His blessings and graces which the Son who was sent by the Father brings to us, everything the Son offers us gratuitously. In the first place, it is what the Father offers us in the Son. God's gift is the gift which the Father makes of His Son to man.

And this water of which Jesus speaks to the Samaritan woman, the water which Jesus gives and which becomes in the believer " a fountain of water, springing up unto life everlasting, "[1] this water is not something of the Saviour's life which is going to be lost in man. Once communicated to man, it goes beyond. It is the very life of Jesus; the whole life of Jesus in so far as directed towards the Father, directed towards that eternal life which is with the Father like the river which rushes towards the ocean; and the impetus of Jesus towards the Father carries man along with it. The countless drops of this flowing follow one after the other. In the faithful soul each blessing calls for another — " and of His fullness we have all received; and grace for grace "[2] — and under the same impulse all these graces converge towards the very object of the Saviour's existence, towards the Father.

[1] Jn 4, 14.
[2] Jn 1, 16.

✣ *XXXVI*

It is in the nature of the Father to draw towards Himself. He draws His Son towards Him. He draws us towards Jesus in order to draw us towards Himself, through Jesus, in Jesus. "No man can come to me except the Father draw him,"[1] says the Saviour. St. Augustine makes a daring parallel between this word about Jesus and the Latin maxim: *trahit sua quemque voluptas* — it is His own delight which draws each one of us. The drawing towards Jesus is the delight which belongs to certain privileged souls. In this way they unite the drawing

[1] Jn 6, 44.

which moves Christ towards His Father who is the joy of the Saviour.

"My meat," says Jesus, "is to do the will of Him that sent Me."[1] The fulfillment of the Father's will is the Saviour's food, for if it were not so, whose image and word would the Son be? The fulfillment of the Father's will through the Saviour's will is our meat because each day this fulfillment renews our strength since it forms and develops the spiritual personality which God assigns to each one of us and because it leads us to full maturity.

In all things Jesus seeks the "glory" of the Father, that is to say, He seeks to manifest the Father. Even when He learns about Lazarus' illness Jesus declares that this sickness is "for the glory of God."[2] The idea of the "glory of God" as the dominant notion of action — an idea so dear to the saints — seems less familiar to Christians of today. Would not the reintegration of this theme in our present-day thinking be exalting and vivifying?

If we want our conception of God's glory to be identified with the one which Jesus had, we will have to look for it in what is considered

[1] Jn 4, 34.
[2] Jn 11, 4.

the inverse of our natural instincts and our psychological habits. We shall also have to reverse some of our values.

Judas left the supper room in order to betray his Master. The Saviour's agony and arrest are near at hand. At this moment Jesus declares : " Now is the Son of Man glorified. " [1] Because from that time the Passion has been offered and virtually accomplished. The decisive act by which Jesus embraces the Passion manifests God's glory; the victorious Resurrection is included in this act. But the Saviour's glorification (and His Father's) is revealed first of all in the acceptance of the redemptive suffering.

---

[1] Jn 13, 31.

✠ *XXXVII*

The Father is profoundly involved in the martyrizing and glorifying decision. "The Father doth love Me," Jesus says, "because I lay down My life."[1] This love of the Father is not explained in the Saviour's statement by the fact that the Father begot the Son, but it is presented to us as caused by the Son's generosity, by His will to be a sacrificial victim. There is in such a phrase a revelation of the Father's being which dazzles and excites.

Jesus even establishes a relationship between His will to sacrifice and His knowledge

[1] Jn 10, 17.

of the Father. " As the Father knoweth Me and I know the Father; and I lay down My life for My sheep. "[1] Knowledge of the Father culminates in the will to sacrifice because God is both love and gift. The martyr has a vital knowledge of God. He is, in a very true sense, the perfect theologian.

Let us consider adoration of the Father: " The hour cometh when you shall neither on this mountain nor in Jerusalem adore the Father... The hour cometh, and now is, when the true adorers shall adore the Father in spirit and in truth. "[2] In these words which Jesus speaks to the Samaritan woman, is there not a decidedly obvious contradiction? If the hour is coming, how can it be here already? If the hour is already here, how is it that it is still to come? And yet the two statements are true.

The hour of pure adoration in spirit and in truth has not yet come, for divisions still continue to exist between those who believe in the same Father, and even between those who believe in the Son. Jesus does not treat these divisions lightly. He does not put the Samaritans and the Jews on the same level.

[1] Jn 10, 15.
[2] Jn 4, 21 ff.

The Samaritans, He says, worship what they do not know, whereas the Jews know what it is they worship, and " salvation is of the Jews. "[1] Likewise, the light of Christ is not kept equally pure by all the groups that claim His friendship. Jerusalem and Garizim still exist.

And meanwhile the hour has already come when the respective sanctuaries are wiped away in the face of adoration in spirit and in truth. For the Samaritan woman, this hour already *is*, it has come, it is present — because at this very moment the Samaritan woman stands before Jesus and opens her soul to Him. The hour of pure adoration has come in so far as Jesus Himself speaks to us and in so far as we listen to Him, for Jesus contains all truth and every man who listens to Jesus and accepts Him clings implicitly to the whole of this truth.

Jesus is the exact image and echo of the Father. What Jesus reveals to us is the Father. And Jesus is revealed to us as the one who is " meek and humble of heart. "[2] We are accustomed to thinking of the Father in terms of power. Yes, the Father is omnipotent.

[1] Jn 4, 22.
[2] Mt 11, 29.

But the Father's heart is meek and humble like the Saviour's. It is meek for in Him there is nothing brusque or abrupt, no violence, no fury, but only kindliness, goodness and affection. His heart is also humble — not that the Father bows before one greater, as the Son become man bows before His Father, but He attaches no importance to display and appearances. He prefers the poor means and is united to the voluntary abasement of His Son who took on our nature and suffering. We must learn to see the Father in this light.

All that Jesus tells us about His own heart is rightfully applied to the heart of the Father. The Father's heart is the model which the heart of Jesus reproduces. Perhaps the most satisfying image we are capable of forming of the Father is that of a heart, the first emotion which is diffused everywhere, the first love which moves all things, the stars and souls. Every beat of that heart is an impulse by which the Father gives Himself. These heartbeats send forth to us the Son's blood, vitalized by the breath of the Spirit.

The Father is heart. To live according to the Father's will is to live subject to this heart, to unite every one of our heartbeats with those of the divine heart.

The Word became man, and this is why, for the first time, a man's heart beats in perfect unison with God's heart. For the first time perfect love for the Father makes a human heart beat. In Jesus Christ is found the perfect fulfillment of human destiny. For the first time a man's heart beats with a perfect love for men. This is the supreme achievement of human destiny — in Christ Jesus this achievement lasts, will last forever as the God-Man Himself. In Jesus, true God and true Man, remains inscribed the vocation of every man. Before He took flesh, the Son loved men with a perfect love. Yet, God's heart was still not united to a human heart.

It is still in the discourse after the Last Supper that Jesus, after speaking of the Father, speaks of the Spirit. Both have their place in these last bursts of love and light. We cannot become intimate with the Son without finding the Father and, at the same time, the Spirit. John had already seen the dove [1] descend upon Jesus when he announced the lamb of God. [2] The lamb and the dove are distinct and inseparable.

[1] Jn 1, 32.
[2] Jn 1, 29.

IC XC

IN ANOTHER FORM

✣ *XXXVIII*

The Holy Spirit descends upon Jesus in the form of a dove.[1] In this way two aspects of the relationship of the Spirit to Jesus come to light. On the one hand, the Spirit descends as the gift of the Father offered to Jesus. On the other hand, the Spirit points out Jesus to men; He introduces Him to them. The Spirit is descent, condescendence, gift. He also manifests the well-beloved Son.

Jesus describes the Spirit's ministry in this way : " He shall not speak of Himself; but what things soever He shall hear, He shall speak... He shall receive of Mine and shall show it to you."[2]

[1] Mt 3, 16.
[2] Jn 16, 13 ff.

Jesus is the Word. Every divine word we hear comes from the Word. The Father has a thought and His thought is expressed and pronounced by the Word. And what is the Spirit? The Spirit is the breath which bears the words. He is the voice which conveys the Word. He is the tongue of fire. The voice has different modulations. The Holy Spirit adapts, accentuates, shades the divine Word according to the needs of all those who hear it. He creates in the same text many appropriate contexts. He interprets the Word by giving it this or that tonality, by surrounding it with this or that atmosphere. He makes it specifically ours. He individualizes it. He is the supreme artist who knows how to accompany the same phrase with infinitely varied harmonizations.

For example, in playing a musical composition, different artists give different degrees of loudness or softness to the same notes. So also in the Semitic languages the vowel signs introduce several variations within the radicals which are only made up of consonants.

In each case the Spirit takes what belongs to Jesus and announces it to us. He says nothing which comes from Himself.

And yet does not the Scripture attribute certain words to the Spirit? Yes it does, but if, for example, in the Acts of the Apostles it happens that the Spirit gives to a prophet, to an apostle, a precise order, it is because everything which depends on the will, on action, is attributed, is appropriated to Him. But these commands of the Spirit are always brief. What the Logos says to the intellect these commandments change into motion of the will. The Spirit does not develop, does not explain. He condenses and repeats what He hears from the Son. Most often He emphasizes it without words. The language of the Holy Spirit is the fervor which He creates.

" I have yet many things to say to you, but you cannot bear them now. But when He, the Spirit of truth, is come... " [1] Jesus repeats to us this word which He had spoken to the apostles. They were not capable of understanding all of Christ's words because the Holy Spirit had not yet been given to them. Now that the Holy Spirit has come, other difficulties can prevent us from understanding the Saviour's word: our indifference, our inattention, our lukewarmness. But He who speaks and His marvelous interpreter remain always within our reach, ready for us to hear.

[1] Jn 16, 12 ff.

At every moment the Spirit speaks to us the words of Jesus, sometimes with the force of a hurricane, and sometimes with the mildness of a light breeze or a babbling brook. But we " grieve the holy Spirit of God "[1] by not listening to Him, by drowning His voice, by driving Him back. Our rudeness becomes impervious to this subtle kindness, to this delicate insistence. It is not capable of sensing the rustling of the dove's wings. This is the eternal Passion of the Holy Spirit, the wounded dove.

The Spirit wants to communicate the Word to us. He effaces Himself in the presence of the Word. And if we try to attain the Spirit independently of the Word — the Spirit without Jesus, the dove without the lamb — the Spirit in some way vanishes. He allows Himself to be felt and grasped only in conjunction with Jesus.

The Spirit is so much a part of our interior life that He becomes, as it were, the " I " of our spiritual life. He speaks in our name. It is He within us who cries : " Abba, Father! "[2] He puts Jesus before us and He unites us to

---

[1] Eph 4, 30.
[2] Rom 8, 15.

the Saviour. It would seem, with all the particulars and reservations which are imposed, that the Son, in whom we become sons of the Father by adoption, is the *object* of the life of our soul and that the Holy Spirit is its *subject*. For the Spirit is identified with what is most profound in us and He makes us reach out towards Jesus.

We must be identified with the descent of the dove which the Father sends to His only begotten Son. We must rest and fasten ourselves on the beloved Son. And in the Son, through the Spirit, we must find the Father, by identifying ourselves with the Saviour's reaching " towards the Father, " as far as such identifications are possible for a creature....

✣ *XXXIX*

It is still, indeed it is always, during the discourse after the Last Supper that Jesus, having spoken of His life with the Father and the Spirit, points out what is His life with His disciples. For there is a relationship of dependence between these two themes. Profound analogies exist between the interweaving of the lives of Father and Son and those of Jesus and His disciples.

"I am in the Father and the Father in Me..."[1] If we consider the union of the Father and the Son in the divine, eternal order, what strikes us especially is the presence of

[1] Jn 14, 11.

Jesus " in the Father. " If we consider still more their union in the divine work, in the order of created beings, our attention is more particularly called to the fact that the Father is present and acting " in Jesus. "

Likewise, Jesus tells us : " You are in Me and I am in you. "[1] In the eternal order, it is especially our incorporation in Jesus — in the body of Christ — which is distinctly marked. In the temporal, historical order, in the sphere of action and obedience it is the work of Jesus in us and through us which seems to be more in evidence.

The evangelist who has reported to us the most affectionate words which Jesus spoke to His own followers is the " disciple whom Jesus loved. "[2] And it is because he was reclining his head on the Master's bosom that this disciple was able to hear what Jesus said in a low voice about the traitor.[3] Jesus reveals His mysteries in a confidential dialogue only to those whose attitude is one of intimate and loving abandonment.

Intimacy with Christ is worth being sought after for itself, in itself. Certainly the light of

[1] Jn 14, 20.   [2] Jn 20, 2.
[3] Jn 21, 20.

the Master, quite in keeping with this intimacy, must brighten the whole landscape and reveal the practical steps which are absolutely essential. We feel disturbed when we see that certain people, qualified as " mystics, " seem to remain indifferent to injustices and cruelties, which though very close to them, would overtake other men. A purely sentimental, emotional piety is not intimacy with Christ. But does not the search after effectiveness, of a worthwhile gesture, of an apparently " productive " sacrifice prevent even certain, very devout, contemporary disciples from understanding the gratuitous breaking of a jar of precious ointment for the Saviour's feet? " To what purpose is this waste? "[1] True, but " he that shall lose his life... "[2]

The Samaritan woman believes that, when the Messias comes, He will teach all things. Jesus answers : " I am He, who am speaking with thee. "[3] The use of the Greek word suggests the idea of an intimate conversation : " I who converse, I who chat with thee... " There is a striking contrast between the free exchange of conversation which the word indicates

[1] Mt 26, 8. [2] Mt 10, 39.
[3] Jn 4, 26.

and the solemn formula " I am, " frequent in the divine statements of the Old Testament. Jesus reveals Himself to us as Lord and Saviour — " I am He " — but He sends us on the way to this revelation by simple, loving dialogues. " I who converse with thee... "

We see the same contrast in the episode of the cure of the man born blind.

" Dost thou believe in the Son of God? — Who is He, Lord, that I may believe in Him? — Thou hast both seen Him; and it is He that talketh with thee. " [1] He who converses familiarly with you is the sublime and far-off figure who is so much awaited. The Son of Man wishes to speak with you man to man. He is beyond, above all things; yet see how He brings Himself down to your level.

Intimacy. The night is falling; the air is getting cooler. My life is coming to an end. It is the hour described by the Canticle of Canticles. [2] Come, my beloved, in the coolness of the evening. Go into the garden. Let the wind, let the breath of your Spirit pass over the flowers which you sowed there yourself and spread their fragrance.

[1] Jn 9, 37 ff.
[2] Ct 4, 16.

Your flowers are always plentiful in other peoples' gardens. But as for me, I have no flowers in my garden. I trampled your uprooted flowers underfoot. I have allowed them to be consumed by the sweltering heat. I have produced brambles. They have formed a part of the crown of thorns which stained my Saviour's head with blood.

Oh, that your flowers might live again! Grant that they may spring up and bloom miraculously under your inspiration. May the loved one be able once again to breathe in the evening their fragrance in His garden.

✞   XL

" Peace I leave with you; My peace I give unto you. "[1] Jesus gives His peace. He does not loan it; He does not take it back. The peace which is in Jesus, " My peace, " becomes the disciples' final possession. At the beginning of each day it is possible for me to be confirmed in the Saviour's peace, no matter what anxieties the day brings.

The Saviour gives His disciples His peace just at the moment when His Passion is about to begin. When He is confronted with the vision of immediate suffering and death, He proclaims and communicates His peace. If at

[1] Jn 14, 27.

such moments Jesus is the Master of Peace, then the strength of this peace will not abandon the disciple in moments of lesser strife.

"But I say to you not to resist evil."[1] How scandalous and foolish is this statement in the eyes of men and especially of unbelievers. How do we interpret these precepts — about turning the left cheek to the one who struck the right, giving our cloak to the one who took our tunic, walking two miles with the one who forced us to go one, giving a blessing to him who curses us? Have we thoroughly explored the ways and means of loving our enemy — whether he be a personal or public one? "You know not of what spirit you are..."[2]

No, it is a question of resisting the Gospel. The choice is not between fighting and not fighting, but between fighting and suffering — and by suffering, conquering. Fighting brings about only vain and illusory victories since Jesus is absolute reality. Suffering without resistance proclaims the absolute reality of Jesus. Understood in this light, suffering is then a real victory. Jesus said: "It is

[1] Mt 5, 39.
[2] Lk 9, 55.

enough," [1] when His disciples presented Him two swords. The disciples had not understood the meaning of Christ's statement : " He that hath not [a purse], let him sell his coat and buy a sword." [2] What Jesus meant was : there are times when we must sacrifice what seems the most ordinary thing, in order to concentrate our attention on the assaults of the evil one. But defense and attack are both spiritual.

Jesus goes out to the front of the troop which, with its torches and arms, wants to lay hands on Him. [3] He goes freely, spontaneously, to His passion.

Jesus cures the servant whose right ear had been cut off by the sword of a disciple. [4] Not only is Jesus unwilling that His disciple defend Him by force : " Suffer ye thus far," [5] He said — but He repairs the damage which the sword had caused. It is the only miracle which Jesus performed during His passion.

The example of non-resistance which Jesus gave does not mean that He consents to evil or that He remains merely passive. It is a positive reaction. It is the reply of the love

[1] Lk 22, 38.
[2] Lk 22, 36.
[3] Jn 18, 4.
[4] Mt 26, 51.
[5] Lk 22, 51.

which Jesus incarnates — opposed to the enterprises of the wicked. The immediate result seems to be the victory of evil. In the long run, the power of this love is the strongest. The Resurrection followed the Passion. The non-resistance of the martyrs wore out and captivated the persecutors themselves. It is the shedding of blood which has guaranteed the spread of the Gospel. Is this a weak and vague pacifism? No, it is a burning and victorious flame. If Jesus, at Gethsemani, had asked His Father for the help of twelve legions of angels, there would have been no Easter or Pentecost.

✠ XLI

"There are eunuchs who have made themselves eunuchs for the Kingdom of Heaven. He that can take, let him take it."[1] The use of the Greek word "take" is stronger than "understand." Jesus agrees to the disciples' opinion: "If the case of a man with his wife be so, it is not expedient to marry. All men take not this word; but they to whom it is given."[2] The Saviour's thought is expressed discreetly but clearly. At the marriage feast of Cana[3] Jesus blessed the union of man and woman. But, to certain ones, it is

[1] Mt 19, 12. [2] Mt 19, 10 ff.
[3] Jn 2, 1.

given to be bethrothed to Jesus alone and to have Him as their one and only spouse.

My child, I belong to you, you belong to Me. Repeat the same sentiments as often as possible. "You belong to Me. I belong to you." Feed yourself on these words. In spite of your past life, in spite of your infidelities, won't you begin now to make every day our bethrothal day? I spoke to you today intimately and at length. Go back now to your fellow men, but keep our secret to yourself.

The voice is becoming clearer: "Behold, the bridegroom cometh. Go ye forth to meet Him."[1] He is about to arrive. Wake up, O my soul, for you have been one of the foolish virgins. Your lamp is going out. Where will you find oil to revive the flame? There is not enough time to buy any. Will the door of the dining room be closed on you? O Jesus, I shall ask You for oil at this last minute. I deserve nothing but Your refusal. But I do not rely on any merit which may be mine. I trust only in Your mercy. I can no longer buy oil; give me freely, then, some of Your oil.

[1] Mt 25, 6.

Death is the dawn when the true sun rises. It is a meeting with the Bridegroom. I go forth to meet Him, to see His face. I throw myself into His arms. Will He take any notice of me if I seek refuge in Him? He is standing on the shore as He did once before in the morning — waiting for His disciples.

No, death is by no means an encounter with Jesus; it is a broadening of vision. Even before my death I must stay close to Him and repose in His embrace. It is in His arms that I must travel through this vale of tears. But at the end of it I shall no longer be blind; I shall see the one who is carrying me. I shall see very clearly what I once felt during the night so obscurely.

Your beloved will lead you to the point where He will reveal Himself to you.

"If any man will come after Me, let him deny himself and take up his cross, and follow Me."[1] The three phases of the disciple's conversion are: renouncement, bearing the cross, walking in the footsteps of the Master.

My child, first of all renounce everything which belongs to you.

Master, I give You everything.

[1] Mt 16, 24.

It is not enough to give Me all that you possess, my child. It is you that I long for. Give Me your heart.

Lord, I give You my heart. Take my heart and my whole being.

Now, My child, take up your cross. Not the one you might imagine or long for, but the one which I shall place on your shoulders.

Master, I accept all the crosses which You wish me to bear. Give me the strength to bear them.

My child, do not say " crosses " as though there were several. There is only My cross; and your cross is Mine suited to you, to your strength. Some people speak of " small crosses. " There are no small crosses. Whatever form it may take, it is My cross which you must bear.

Master, I shall bear it, if You give me the strength.

My child, it is not enough to take up your cross and walk behind Me. It is true that it is by bearing the cross that one really does follow Me. But you must follow Me right to the end. You know where I am going; I am going to Golgotha. The cross which I am carrying and which you are carrying is the instrument of a life immolated unto death.

After carrying the cross you will have to stretch out on it, be nailed to it, and die on it. Are you willing to stay with Me right to the end? Are you willing to carry My cross up to Calvary? And once you get there, don't you want to share in My crucifixion?

Master, I have not the strength to be crucified with You.

My child, he that shall lose his life for My sake shall find it.[1] I know that you are not ready. The sacrifice attracts you; but you are not yet capable of it. I would like to prepare you for it, day by day. Every morning be ready to embrace the cross which the new day sets before you. Accept it in the spirit of the total immolation of Golgotha, as one more step towards the end of the *via dolorosa*.

[1] Cfr. Mt 16, 25.

✤ *XLII*

Before His passion Jesus raised His eyes to Heaven and said: "Father, the hour is come."[1] Jesus waited for the time which His Father had established. Now the moment has come. The fulfillment of the divine will demands acceptance at the appointed time. All delay and haste are excluded.

During His agony at Gethsemani, when an angel appears to Jesus to strengthen Him,[2] His cup is not removed. The Angel strengthens Jesus so that Jesus will accept the cup.

[1] Jn 17, 1.
[2] Lk 22, 43.

On two occasions when Jesus gave His name to the soldiers, they drew back and fell to the ground.[1] Their prostration means that Jesus is stronger than they, and that it is by His own free choice that He gives Himself up.

None of the Saviour's harsh words to the Scribes and Pharisees, against the " generation of vipers, "[2] the " wrath of the Lamb, "[3] appears in the Passion. The more Jesus suffers, the more He proves that He is kind and merciful.

Master, You do not love men less when You suffer on their account than You loved them before You suffered. Even though You hate my sin, it is while I sin that You love me most anxiously.

Jesus, in His passion, " began to grow sorrowful and to be sad. "[4] His human nature knows from experience all the attacks, all the agitations to which our nature is liable. His divine nature, however, remains in perfect peace, the divine peace of a soul humanly " sorrowful even unto death. "[5] The old teaching of the Councils on the two natures of Christ, distinct but without separation, united in the same

[1] Jn 18, 5 ff.
[2] Mt 23, 33.
[3] Ap 6, 16.
[4] Mt 26, 37.
[5] Mt 26, 38.

person, is not a contention about words nor a vain subtlety. It is this doctrine which warrants our belief that in Jesus both the divine and the human remain wholly integral and yet they are united with each other. The storm may strike the foot of a mountain but the summit is in full sunlight.

" Greater love than this no man hath, that a man lay down his life for his friends. "[1] In this statement is contained the most complete, most profound explanation of the Saviour's passion. The greatest love is the highest possible kind. It demands a giving of oneself which continues right unto death. Golgotha is not a requirement of justice, but one of love.

Master, I stand at the foot of Your cross, with Mary, Your mother, with the disciple whom You loved, with the women who remained faithful to You.[2]

I am bold enough to lift up my eyes to You and in this look cast on Your sacrifice, I am learning what I did not know how to learn through the very words of the Gospel.

Your feet are nailed to the wood. Your cross is the winepress where the true vine is

[1] Jn 15, 13.
[2] Jn 19, 25.

pressed. You have no possibility of escape. You are waiting for me at the rendezvous which You have assigned to me. Fastened to the cross, You compel yourself to this waiting. It is possible for me *not* to come, but You are there and You remain where You have allowed Yourself to be placed.

Your arms are stretched out. They are opened as an appeal to all men. They cannot be closed again. The nails keep them there in this gesture which is at one and the same time an invitation and an embrace. In silence they beckon to me : " Come. "

Your head hangs low. You bow it in a motion of acquiescence. You have accepted and consummated God's will, therefore Yours, in so far as it is also the Father's and the Spirit's. You bow Your head as a sign of obedience to what the love of the Three requires towards men.

At the same time Your head is bowed towards those who are there below. It is bowed towards those who loved You, towards those who cried out : " Crucify Him!, " [1] towards those who suffer, and linger on, groaning, towards those who seek without being aware of it.

[1] Jn 19, 15.

Your eyes are closed now. In one and the same interior vision they see the Father and men, and the movement of Your whole being is directed towards these two objects of Your love.

Blood flows from Your forehead, from Your hands, and from Your scourged body. It flows slowly in long streams, it is going to flow from Your open side as though Your heart were bursting under the pressure of Your suffering love. The cup is poured out in a libation.

The crown of thorns bruised Your head. Woven in the form of a circle these thorns are like the sins of men, gathered together and heaped upon You. All the sins of men are contiguous and bound together. The Jewish priest, stretching forth his hands, placed these sins on the victim's head. In this way men have placed with their own hands the circle of their sins on the noblest part of Your body — on Your head.

But around this head, I see rays of light. A golden halo emanates from Your blood-stained head. This moisture gives its meaning to the painful vision. If I did not notice it, I would have only an incomplete picture of the Crucified. The Crucified is also Lord and Saviour.

Jesus, in front of Your cross, I cannot speak anymore; I cannot even think anymore. I look at You and at each breath, at each heartbeat I would like Your image to penetrate more deeply. Enter then, into me, O shining Crucified One! Come, O crucified Lord, come and be nailed to my body. Nail Yourself to my soul. Grant that I may carry You with me forever, pressing You to me, You, the loved one.

They will not understand; they will speak of a morbid imagination. But we are together.

I belong to You. I belong to You. I am wholly in Your hands. I can only stammer and repeat those words. Be the seal on my heart, on my senses. May that familiar picture of Your arms outstretched on the cross never eave me and may it save me in times of temptation! Grant that I may never break or tarnish it, and may its permanence in me allow me in my last agony to approach, trembling but joyful, the moment of my death.

Master, Your passion has not ended. Your wounds are still bleeding. They are still crucifying You this very day. Where? One has only to read the newspapers. Your body is tortured, crucified everywhere, at all times, in Your human members.

" Were you there when they crucified my Lord? " This line from a negro spiritual asks a very real and poignant question. Am I there where they crucify my Lord? Am I capable of developing, according to the dimensions of the universal, present-day Golgotha, my poor imagination which is so narrow, so centered on itself? Can I make myself present in the agonies of Christ's body which are felt by every man whom the devil seeks to devour, agonies often caused by men, sometimes in Your name, O Christ? Can I make myself present at Christ's intimate conversation with every unfortunate person? An intimate conversation? Yes, on the one hand a human head, and on the other the Holy Face, bruised and ridiculed? I shall be present at these conversations if I carry within me the image of that Holy Face.

✠ XLIII

Let us consider the permanence and reality of the Saviour's Passion. They have bound His hands for the sake of our freedom. He fights with us and for us. He is often wounded. Sometimes He seems to be dead within a soul. The way in which He knows and understands all human suffering is a far deeper and more intimate identification with this suffering than any extraneous sympathy or pity; it goes even deeper than the conscience which suffers as a result of its own pains. For Jesus knows from within and not from without. He not only has foreknowledge but complete comprehension. His knowledge takes and makes its own what is known — just like a hot iron which has reddened to white makes its own the fire into which it is plunged. As God, Jesus is the Being from whom we have our being. He *is* Being; we only have being. His Being is interior to all beings, more interior to a man than a man is to himself, and without ever confusing the Creator with the created. It is because of His own divine Being that everything that is, everything that happens to man, even suffering and sin, receives the possibility of existence. Human suffering, as a negative aspect of being, has therefore its roots in the very Being of God. Certainly God condemns evil in all its forms, but He knows men's pain as no other man will ever know it. As God He knows it from within His own Being whence all being derives and because to know suffering in this way is to enter into it.

Master, does Your divine perfection exclude all suffering? Obviously it excludes suffering in the human sense which implies limitation, privation and violation of one's integrity. It also excludes suffering imposed by an external force. Man is able to suffer, but You, Master, cannot be crushed or limited by anything or anyone. Nevertheless, instead of considering that a decrease of divine perfection has somehow been imposed on God and accepted by Him, we could conceive that God willingly, actively, of His own initiative, takes on Himself man's suffering. The act by which God would assume human suffering would be a free act of His sovereignty, an act diminishing nothing of the divine perfection. It is true that such an act could not outwardly diminish Your perfection, O divine Master, but it could burst it. I use the words "outwardly" and "burst" because it is a question of a kind of explosion by which a certain order of being, a certain perfection would develop and give place to the irruption of another form of perfection, which is not essentially superior to the first, but superior in so far as it is at this moment preferred and desired by God. If this is so, O my Saviour, could one not say (oh!, certainly in a vague kind of way and with trembling lips) that You are capable of suffering without ceasing to be perfect, without any diminution imposed on Your resurrected and glorified life? Your suffering would simply be the expression of Your divine love freely creating its own burden.

Your Passion, O Master, is an historical fact, but it goes beyond history. It belongs to Your own time, to the time of Christ. We who live in a world of successive events are tempted to introduce the notion of succession in our conception of divine life. But You, My God, transcend events and history : You are eternal. Not that Your eternity is a continual series, a line extended to infinity. Your divine eternity is rather a unique point in which all is present. The past and the future are mixed up in it with the very instant which we are now living. In You, Master, there is a complete presence of being. The totality of succession in time is dissolved in the unity of a now which transcends all the before's and after's of our human experience. Our human time, O Godman, has been carried off by You to heaven, into divine eternity. Your eternity contains within itself every moment of human time, past and future. All that human suffering which You took with You on the Cross, and your crucifixion itself, are more than just events in time. Good Friday and Easter make one event in the eternity of Your divine life, even though, historically, the Passion precedes the Resurrection. It is through suffering that God triumphs over suffering. Your suffering, O Christ, is not opposed to Your glory and Your beatitude. It is the very matter from which You draw your eternal triumph. Your suffering, simultaneous with Your victory, *is* overcome, illuminated and transfigured by it. Such tears as Yours, fervent joy would dry immediately; suffering conceived in this way would be the fuel which feeds a consuming fire.

Do I still dare to say, O my Saviour, that You have been not only a suffering God, but that You are still so, that Your present suffering is a mystery which I may speak of only by analogy and approximation? If I say that you still suffer now, it is because I know no other words which are capable of expressing this reality which I intuitively feel. When I say : " Jesus suffers, " I do not mean to describe the same experience as the one which the words " I suffer " convey. Is it then simply a manner of speaking, a metaphor? Certainly not, for I believe, O Jesus, that Your present suffering is a reality quite as much and even more than man's suffering. But I do not think of Your suffering in terms of human suffering. I say that you suffer — because these words are the only translation (miserably inadequate though it be) of something which exists in God. It is something which even now in You corresponds, in an ineffable and transcendent way, to the suffering of creation.

Why then do I persist in considering this theme? Why do I persist in looking for words which I know are only wretched mumbling? Does all that have any real importance for our life today? I believe so, deeply. If we accept it, if we meditate on it (O Master, grant that this message may be true!), on the good news of the suffering Christ who is still with us, but whose suffering is already surmounted — although we did not see it — then human suffering becomes mitigated. Suffering souls are better disposed to the promises of joy. To the mother who has just lost her only son, to the young wife who has just lost her husband, we can say : " Jesus Himself, at this very moment, is suffering what you are suffering, and He triumphs over it for you forever. The cross which you are carrying, as Simon of Cyrene carried it, is your Saviour's cross. Jesus carries it at this moment with you. You do not yet see that this bearing of the cross by you two together expresses a triumph. Your eyes will be opened and you will see. "

The Saints have always felt that the Saviour's passion was not a simple event of the past. They made themselves contemporaries of it in a sort of way; they were not concerned about reconciling Christ's beatitude after the

Ascension with His present sufferings. These things are unprovable. Let's go back to St. Augustine's way of putting it: *Da mihi amantem et sentit quod dico:* Give me someone who loves and he will feel what I am saying.

The Father and the Spirit each take that part in the Son's passion which is proper to Him. All three of them obey the demands of love made on them by their common essence. The Father supports the Saviour's cross with His own hands; and the dove hovers over them. There was a cross in God's heart before it was set up outside the walls of Jerusalem. The wooden cross has been taken away, but the one which was in the divine heart is still there. The Lamb has been immolated since the foundation of the world." He does not stop being immolated.

" Put in thy finger hither and see My hands; and bring hither thy hand and put it into My side. "[1] There is in these words more than an invitation to Thomas to prove the truth of the Saviour's bodily resurrection.

My child, see My wounds. All those who cry out against the truth, would like to reduce

[1] Jn 20, 27.

My Gospel to a thing of wisdom or to an ideal. I am the Saviour who died on the cross. To all those who are willing to hear about the victory, Resurrection, Transfiguration, but who would like to ignore Golgotha, My wounds are reminders that the cross is a necessary condition for salvation.

My wounds have also another meaning. Since My Ascension, you can touch My pierced hands and My open side only if you bend down in compassion over the wounds of men. In times of doubt, look for someone lower than yourself. Comfort that unfamiliar pain. I am the One you will touch. My living presence will become certain for you in this contact with the suffering members of My body.

XLIV

It is Easter morning and the women who are on their way to the sepulchre at daybreak, carrying spices, are saying to one another: " Who shall roll us back the stone? "[1] For a stone which is very big blocks the entrance of the tomb. According to all human reckoning, it is improbable that the women will be able to get to the Saviour's body.

Jesus often seems imprisoned in my soul and reduced to helplessness, as He was in the sepulchre before the Resurrection. The heavy stone of my sin keeps Him in that state. How

[1] Mk 16, 3.

many times I have longed to see Jesus rise in me in His light and power! How many times have I tried to roll back the stone — but in vain! The weight of sin, the weight of its habits were too strong. I would say to myself almost in despair: " Who will roll the stone back? "

Nevertheless, the women are on their way to the tomb. Their approach is a pure act of faith. This faith — this madness — will have its reward. I too must persist in this mad hope that the stone will be removed.

But the women going to the tomb are not empty-handed. They bring spices bought in order to embalm the Saviour's body. [1] If I long for the stone to be removed from my soul, I must — at least as a sign, a token of my good will — bring something with me. Perhaps it would be very little, but it must be something which cost me something, something which is in the nature of a sacrifice.

Now the women find that the stone at the entrance of the sepulchre has been removed, It has been removed in a way which they had not foreseen. " There was a great earthquake. For an angel of the Lord descended from

[1] Mk 16, 1.

heaven and coming rolled back the stone." [1] In order to remove the stone, nothing less than a cataclysm was necessary. A push, a slight readjustment would not be enough. Likewise, the stone which seems to immobilize and paralyze Jesus in my soul can be taken away only by an earthquake, that is to say, by a violent interior catastrophe, by a complete and radical change. A jolt like lightning is required to unsettle me. Jesus rises from the dead in me only if the one who I was ceases to exist, giving way to the new man. Not a retouching or a tuning up will do; but a death and a birth are necessary.

The angel annouces to the disciples that the risen Christ is waiting for them in Galilee. Jesus Himself renews this order: " Go, tell My brethren that they go into Galilee. There they shall see Me." [2] Why this return to Galilee? Does Jesus want to protect His disciples from the enmity of the Jews? Does He want to assure them, after the anxieties of His Passion, of days of peace and calm? Perhaps. But there seems to be an even deeper reason.

[1] Mt 28, 2.
[2] Mt 28, 10.

It was in Galilee that the disciples had met Jesus. There they had heard the call and begun to follow the Saviour. The memory of those days was to preserve in their souls a springtime freshness. After the infidelities of the previous week, Jesus wanted to plunge His disciples once again into that first freshness, that first fervor. He wanted to renew in them the emotion, the decision of the first meeting. In the Galilean atmosphere which He brings to life again, He will complete His revelation.

There is a Galilee in the life of each one of us — or at least in the life of those among us, who, one day, met the Saviour and loved Him. This Galilee is, in my period of existence, the time when I became aware that Jesus was looking at me, and calling me by name. Since then, many years have gone by. These years could be laden with countless sins. It may seem that I have forgotten Jesus Christ. Yet, whoever has met Jesus just once cannot forget Him. Jesus invites me to go back to the Galilee of my soul, to bring to life again within me the intimacy and fervor of the first days. There, again I shall see Him.

Master, I would like to go back to Galilee. But will I meet You there? How can I warm up my heart which has become so cold? Will the memory of our Galilee be enough to recreate the emotion of our first meeting?

" He will go before you into Galilee... " [1] My child, you will not have to evoke My presence painfully. I shall be faithful to the appointment which I have made with you. I shall do more than wait for you in this Galilee of memories. Now I go before you, I shall lead you there. When your heart is once again fixed on Galilee, the One who is guiding you will make Himself known to you, and He will speak to you...

[1] Mt 28, 7.

✣ XLV

After His Resurrection Jesus suddenly appeared in the midst of His disciples. He does not linger over long reproaches on their infidelity and unbelief. And they do not waste time over long excuses or explanations. Everything happens so simply, so familiarly : " Have you here anything to eat? " [1]

" They offered Him a piece of a broiled fish and a honeycomb. " [2] Life goes on again in normal conditions, at the very point where it had been interrupted.

[1] Lk 24, 41.
[2] Lk 24, 42.

When I have betrayed and abandoned Jesus, it is not necessary that I anxiously look for and prepare the conditions for my repentant encounter with the Master. I must only reintroduce Jesus into my daily life, put Him in the present context, involve Him in the difficulties and hopes of the moment. The gesture is sufficient, by which we offer Jesus His share of the fish and honey which are our daily nourishment. Right away Jesus is going to resume His place at our table and share our life again. That will come about in an instant; but as far as we are concerned, it must be done in humility and repentance. The exterior attitude will be simple and easy. Yet it must be characterized by an interior prostration.

" After that He appeared in another shape... "[1] After His Resurrection Jesus appears to those who have known Him,[2] but under new forms so that they do not recognize Him at once. Mary, near the sepulchre, took Him for the gardener.[3] On the road to Emmaus, the two disciples took Him for a traveller.[4] The Apostles who were fishing did not know who this stranger was, standing on the shore

---

[1] Mk 16, 12.   [2] Jn 20, 20.
[3] Jn 20, 15.   [4] Lk 24, 13 ff.

of the lake,[1] until John says to Peter: "It is the Lord."[2]

Why all these changes in our Saviour's appearance? Jesus wants to indicate that His physical presence is no longer localized, as it was before His Resurrection, in a definite place, bound to a specific form. His presence is no longer limited. It has become universal as to place and form. His glorified body can be approached everywhere by everyone.

There is still more. Jesus appears several times in the form of a stranger in order to point out that, henceforth, when the historical Christ has ascended into Heaven, it is with human features easily recognized by us that His divine nature will be clothed. Already He declares to His disciples long before His death that He was hungry and thirsty, that He has been naked and sick, a stranger and a prisoner,[3] in those whom we have fed and given to drink, clothed and looked after, received and visited — and in those who were in need of these things and whom we did not help. "As long as you did it to one of these My least brethren, you did it to Me."[4] God and His creatures will never

---

[1] Jn 21, 4.   [2] Jn 21, 7.
[3] Mt 25, 35 ff.   [4] Mt 25, 40.

be identical. We are not Christ by nature, but we are by participation and by grace. We are His members. It is under this form that Jesus becomes visible and tangible to us. To this generation which declares itself realistic and is unwilling to adore a phantom, Jesus says: " See My hands and feet. "[1] Today, on this earth, He has no other hands and no other feet than those of men. If you are unable to climb directly to Jesus through prayer, leave your house and at once you will find Him in the street in the form of the man and woman who are passing by.

In these forms the possibility of an uninterrupted meeting with Jesus is given to us. My Saviour reveals Himself to me at the office, at the workshop, in the department store, on the bus, in the lines of people who stand about waiting and in those who rush on their way. We find Christ in His churches, but it is at the exit of these places called " holy " that He invites us to begin the search and discovery of His person under our brethren's features. To approach Christ in this way in the spirit of humility is both very easy and very difficult — It is easy since Jesus is there in each one of those

[1] Lk 24, 39.

persons who surround us, and it is difficult since what is more common, more ordinary, and more a part of everyday life requires the greatest effort. It is perhaps easier to recognize Christ in the prostitute and in the sinner than in an ordinary, irritating individual. In the latter as in the former, it is a question of liberating " Christ in chains. " On our part an act of faith is required, as well as an act of adoration and of love — an act of personal self-giving — at least in our will, if the opportunity is not given to us to serve in some particular way this Christ who is passing by. At each and every step we can transfigure men if we see in them the often disfigured Holy Face. St. John Chrysostom tells us that the living and human altar set up in every street, in every crossroad is more sacred than a stone altar, because on the second, Christ is offered, but the first is Christ Himself.

XLVI

"Signs," says Jesus, "shall follow them that believe"[1] — not only the disciples, but all those who have accepted the Gospel. Jesus specifies what these signs shall be. In His name believers shall cast out devils. They shall speak in new tongues. They shall cure the sick.

Have we taken this promise seriously? Do we make progress in life, in the world, within the power of Christ? It is a question of faith. These powers will be given to "them that believe." Do I believe this in the

[1] Mk 16, 17.

strong sense which the Gospel gives to this word?

O Jesus my Saviour, " help my unbelief. "[1] Increase my faith, and I venture to add : give me the possibilities which You promised to those who believe, in so far as they would serve Your glory as well as souls. If I ask that, it is in the spirit in which Your apostle Paul desired that everyone have a share in charismatic graces.[2] It is not that I want to enjoy a spiritual power or cause astonishment by means of signs, but to be of help and to bear witness.

Jesus returned to His Father. There where He now is, He wills us to be also. " This day, " He said to the crucified robber, " thou shalt be with Me in paradise. "[3] " With Me " : the Greek text uses here a preposition (not SYN, but META) which implies much more than a simultaneous presence. It implies a destiny which is shared, a common life. It is not enough to say that the robber will be there where Jesus is; he will share in the very life of Jesus.

And so it will be with us, if we follow Christ our Master right to the very end.

[1] Mk 9, 23. [2] 1 Cor 14, 1.
[3] Lk 23, 43.

I shall be able not only to see Him, but to partake of His glorious life. And that can begin right now. " This day... " Paradise can be for me, if not wide open, at least ajar, this very day, in so far as I cling to Christ. The disciple's life is a kind of diptych, since the Master is here below and with the Father at the same time. Heavenly life is only an extension and a deepening of life in Jesus. My life after death will confirm and establish my present choice. This very day, I can begin to be in Paradise with Jesus.

"Whilst He blessed them, He departed from them and was carried up to Heaven."[1] These words describe our relationship with Jesus since His Ascension. "Whilst He blessed them... " The glorified body of the Saviour has been separated from us, carried up next to His Father. But Jesus preserves His ties with us and is involved in our efforts. At the very moment when He ascended He blessed us. A complete vision of the Saviour includes both His Ascension into Heaven and the gesture of blessing which Jesus does not cease to perform over His disciples and their works. This gesture unites Heaven to earth.

[1] Lk 24, 51.

"Follow thou Me."[1] This is the Saviour's last word reported by the Gospels. It is the first word which Jesus, on the shore, spoke to Peter[2] and it is the last word which, still on the shore of the lake, He speaks to him. This word contains all things.

Peter, when he had been called, did not know what " to follow Jesus " implied. Now after the Passion, after his own failings, he understands it better. Nevertheless he will know it perfectly only in his martyrdom. " Another shall gird thee... "[3]

In the evening of life — even of a life of infidelity — as in the morning, Jesus does not cease to utter this same imperative, and merciful call : " Follow thou Me. "

Master, I have so often and for so many years heard the call! How many times I have started on the way! And then I have fallen, I have not continued. I have gotten up again; I have fallen again. I cannot say that I have followed You. I have lost sight of You, and yet I have always felt that You were there...

Get up again. Begin again. But then, You mean, Master, I am not rejected in spite of my innumerable betrayals?

[1] Jn 21, 22. [2] Mt 4, 19.
[3] Jn 21, 18.

Come after Me. Follow Me.

Master, would You grant me, perhaps for the last time, the grace of calling me?

Yes, My child. Do you really want to come?

Master, I am on the way...

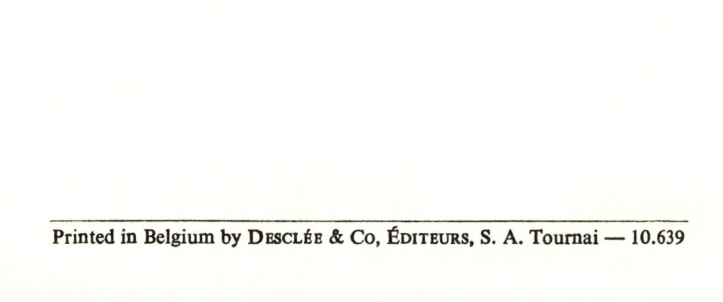

Printed in Belgium by Desclée & Co, Éditeurs, S. A. Tournai — 10.639